Just Right READING

Level D

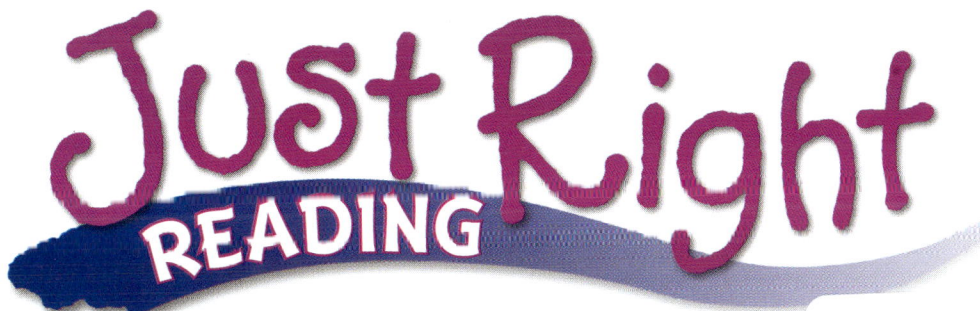

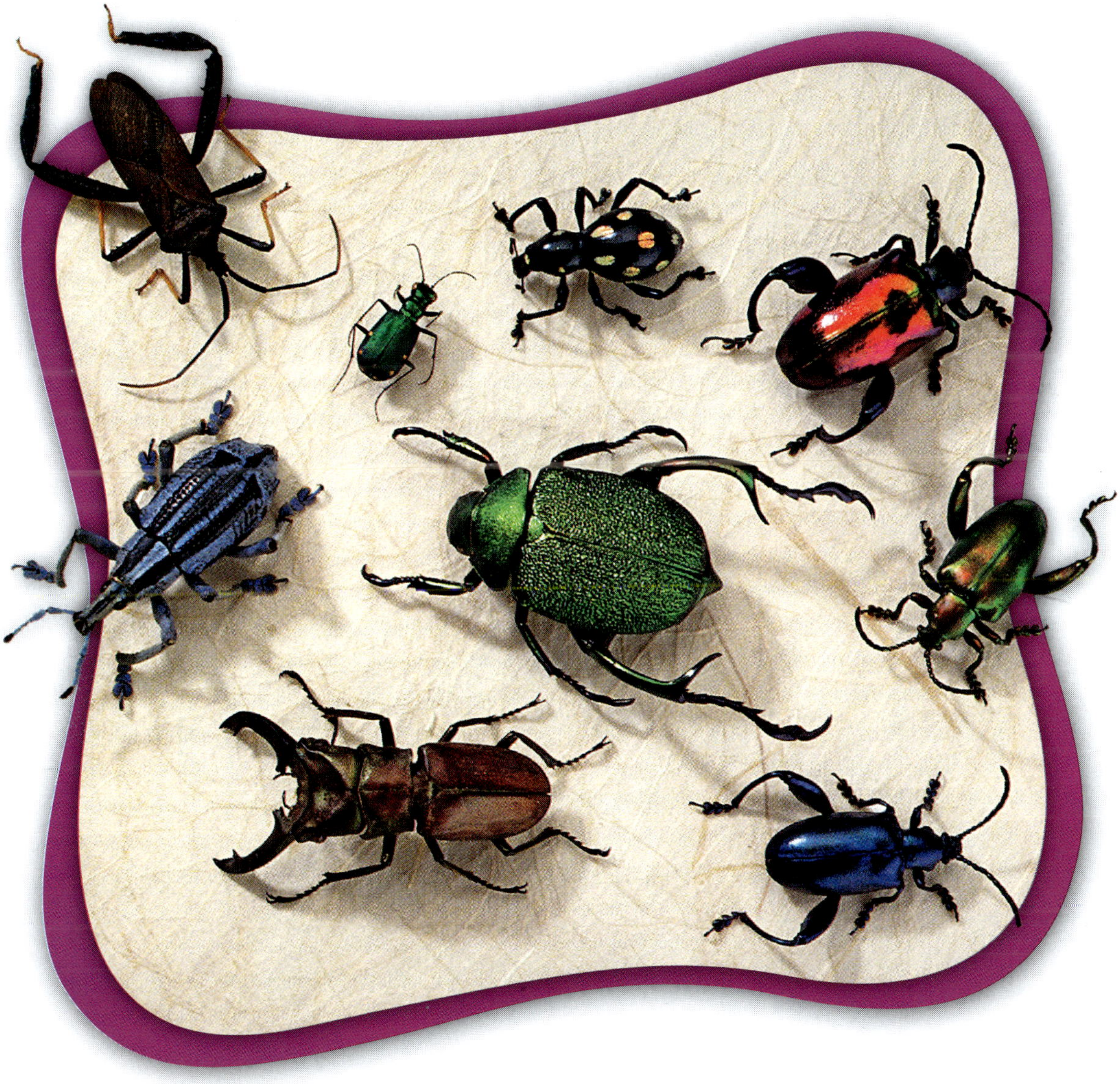

Options Publishing

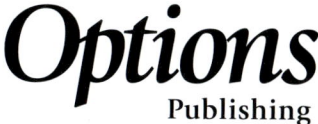

Level D

Acknowledgments

Product Development: The Quarasan Group, Inc.
Cover Design: The Quarasan Group, Inc.
Editor: Wendy Whitnah
Production Supervisor: Sandy Batista

Credits Abbreviations are as follows: t=top, c=center, b=bottom, l=left, r=right

Photos: Cover ©MetaCreations/Kai Power Photos; page 3 ©Neil Fletcher/Dorling Kindersley Picture Library; 4 (t) Courtesy of John Hockenberry, (b) ©Steve Wilkings/Corbis; 5 (t) Apparel courtesy Direct Access International, (b) ©Jack Smith/AP/Wide World Photos; 19 ©MetaCreations/Kai Power Photos; 20 (t) ©PhotoDisc/Punch Stock, (b) ©Janine Wiedel Photolibrary/Alamy Images Ltd.; 22 (c) ©Clemson University-USDA Cooperative Extension Slide Series, (inset) ©Dr. Ken Greer/Visuals Unlimited, Inc.; 23 ©Neil Fletcher/Dorling Kindersley Picture Library; 24 ©Gyorgy Csoka/Hungary Forest Research Institute/Forestry Images; 25 ©Richard Seaman; 26 ©Reuters/Corbis; 27 (r) ©Peter Arnold/Alamy Images, Ltd., (l) ©John T. Fowler/Alamy Images, Ltd.; 28 ©John T. Fowler/Alamy Images Ltd.; 29 ©Neil Fletcher/Dorling Kindersley Picture Library; 30 ©Dr. Robert Calentine/Visuals Unlimited, Inc.; 45 ©Warren Faidley/Weatherstock; 48 ©Michael L. Bak/Department of Defense/Getty Images; 51 all © DigitalGlobe; 52 ©Warren Faidley/Weatherstock; 53 ©Ted Mahieu/Corbis; 55 ©NOAA; 56 ©Gary Braasch/Corbis; 57 ©Steve Wilkings/Corbis; 58, 59, 60 all Courtesy of John Hockenberry; 61 ©AP/Wide World Photos; 62 ©Peter Turnley/Corbis; 63 Courtesy of John Hockenberry; 64 ©Charlie Samuels Photography, Inc.; 65 Courtesy of John Hockenberry; 66 ©Charlie Samuels Photography, Inc.; 67 ©Peter Turnley/Corbis; 68 Courtesy of John Hockenberry; 69 ©Beata Pastuszek/iStock Photo; 70 Courtesy of John Hockenberry; 84 ©Jack Smith/AP/Wide World Photos; 85 ©Mike Cash/AP/Wide World Photos; 87 ©Photo Researchers, Inc.; 88 ©Photo Researchers, Inc.; 89 ©AP/Wide World Photos; 90 © Ron Niebrugge/Alamy Images Ltd., (inset) Courtesy of United States Geological Survey; 91 Courtesy of United States Geological Survey; 92 ©PhotoDisc, Inc.; 93 ©David R. Frazier/Photo Researchers, Inc.; 94 ©Jack Smith/AP/Wide World Photos; 95 Courtesy of United States Geological Survey; 97 ©David Young-Wolff/PhotoEdit, Inc.; 98 ©TNT Magazine/Alamy Images Ltd.; 99 ©Creatas/Punch Stock; 100 Photo courtesy Peter E. Julber, apparel courtesy Cagoule Fleece. 101 ©Wally Eberhart/Visuals Unlimited, Inc.; 102 Apparel courtesy Direct Access International; 103 ©Tom Stillo/Index Stock Imagery; 104 ©PhotoDisc Inc./Punch Stock; 105 ©Diane Diederich/iStockphoto; 106 ©Barbara Stitzer/Photo Edit, Inc.; 107 Photo courtesy Peter E. Julber, apparel courtesy Cagoule Fleece. 108 ©Think Stock/Alamy Images Ltd.; 109 ©David Young-Wolff/PhotoEdit Inc., 113 ©Corbis; 116 ©Michael L. Bak/Department of Defense/Getty Images; 117 ©Jack Smith/AP/Wide World Photos; 118 Courtesy of John Hockenberry; 119 ©Peter Turnley/Corbis.

Illustrations: Cecile Schoberle: 2; Meg Aubrey: 3, 6–18; Bill Melvin: 20–21; Stacey Schuett: 32–43; Cecile Schoberle: 71–83; Cheryl Kirk Noll: 110.

ISBN: 1-59137-524-X

Options Publishing
P.O. Box 1749
Merrimack, NH 03054-1749
TOLL FREE: 800-782-7300 • TOLL FREE FAX: 866-424-4056

www.optionspublishing.com

All rights reserved. Printed in USA.
15 14 13 12 11 10 9 8 7 6 5 4 3 2 1

©2006 Options Publishing. All rights reserved. No part of this document may be reproduced or used in any form or by any means—graphic, electronic, or mechanical, including photocopying, recording, taping, and information storage and retrieval systems—without written permission of the publisher.

Table of Contents

✓ **Lesson 1** Broom Hockey Expert 6

   Comprehension: Cause and Effect
   Word Study: Plural Nouns

Lesson 2 Beetles Everywhere 19

   Comprehension: Main Idea and Details
   Word Study: Verb Endings

✓ **Lesson 3** A Gift of Words 32

   Comprehension: Understanding Characters
   Word Study: Words with Multiple Meanings

Table of Contents

Lesson 4   Tsunamis: Danger from the Sea 45

    Comprehension: Comparing and Contrasting
    Word Study: Adjectives That Compare

Lesson 5   John Hockenberry:
                  Reporting on the World 58

    Comprehension: Fact and Opinion
    Word Study: Synonyms and Antonyms

Lesson 6   The 12-Hour Race 71

    Comprehension: Summarizing
    Word Study: Pronouns

✓**Lesson 7**   A Gray Day in May................84
   Comprehension: Context Clues
   Word Study: Prefixes

Lesson 8   Plastic Fashion 97
   Comprehension: Making Inferences
   Word Study: Suffixes

Review.................................110

Glossary................................116

5

1 Get Ready to Read
Broom Hockey Expert

1 Characters

David
a new student

Ken
David's friend

Ms. Gomez
David's teacher

2 Setting: school playground

3 Vocabulary

newcomer someone who has just come to a place

hesitate pause because of feeling unsure

dribble move a ball forward by bouncing it

shoot throw a ball toward a goal

encourage gently push someone to do something

puzzle to confuse

astonished surprised

constantly all the time

contest a game between two people or teams to win

4 Build Background

- What games or sports do you know how to play?
- How did you learn to play the games?

Broom Hockey Expert

"What if the kids at my new school don't like me?" David asked Mom. Slowly he put on his jacket and his backpack.

"David, just give yourself some time to get used to your new school, and you'll do fine," Mom said, patting him on the shoulder as he went out the door.

As David walked to school, he kept worrying. His family had just moved from Canada to California. He already missed his friends from home and wanted to make new friends quickly. He wanted to fit in, but he was afraid kids in California might like different things than his friends in Canada.

Before he knew it, he was at his new school.

"Welcome!" Ms. Gomez greeted David at the classroom door. "Come in and sit in the desk next to Ken. I have asked Ken to help you get settled today."

Ken smiled at David, and the **newcomer** relaxed a little. Ken seemed very friendly. In fact, all the students were friendly. They made David feel very welcome.

When it was time for lunch, Ken invited David to sit with him and some other boys and girls in the lunchroom. After lunch, a girl named Lisa said, "We are crazy about basketball! We all play at recess and any other time we can. Do you want to play with us?"

David **hesitated.** He liked basketball, but he didn't play it very often. However, he wanted to fit in with his new friends. "Sure," David said, feeling a little nervous.

Recess seemed to go on for hours. David was amazed at the other students' skill. They could **dribble** the ball down the court as fast as lightning. They could **shoot** one basket after another without missing. David did his best, but he knew that he needed a lot more practice. The other children **encouraged** the newcomer to keep trying.

"Give yourself some time to learn," Lisa told him.

"You can do it, David," Ken said.

Every day, the kids played basketball at recess and after school. They always included David in their games. He tried hard, but he was still struggling. "Why don't you come practice at my house after school?" Ken suggested.

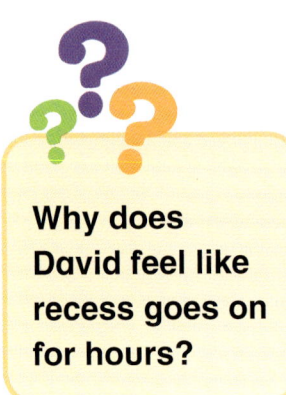

Why does David feel like recess goes on for hours?

David and Ken spent hours practicing. No matter how well David learned to dribble and shoot the ball, he always thought the others did it better.

One Saturday morning, Ken stopped by David's house. He saw something that **puzzled** him. David's father was drawing chalk lines on the driveway. His mother was getting out a bunch of brooms. David and his sister Michelle bounced a ball to each other.

"What are you doing?" Ken asked David.

"We're going to play broom hockey. A lot of people in Canada play it. Do you want to play, too?"

Now Ken was the one who hesitated. He had heard of broom hockey, but he didn't know how to play it. "I'll try," Ken said nervously.

Soon Ken was scrambling to keep up in the lively game. Dad, Michelle, and Ken were on one team, and Mom and David were on the other. The purpose of the game was to use a broom to sweep the ball past the other team's goal line. Of course, the other team tried to keep this from happening.

Ken was **astonished** at how quickly and how well David could sweep the ball past the goal line. He scored many points for his team. Ken, on the other hand, was not able to get the ball past David and his mother even once, but he had fun anyway.

As soon as the other kids saw David walk into the classroom Monday morning, they surrounded him and encouraged him to tell them about broom hockey. Ken had told them how excited he was about learning to play, and they wanted to learn, too. Ms. Gomez asked Mr. Brooks, the man who cleaned the school, if she could borrow some brooms. At recess, David and Ken showed their classmates how to play.

That afternoon, many of the kids went home and asked to borrow brooms. It wasn't long before all the kids in the neighborhood were playing broom hockey. They were **constantly** playing the game or talking about it.

> **Why did Ms. Gomez ask Mr. Brooks for brooms?**

Ms. Gomez was astonished at how excited her students were about the new game. "I'm pleased to see you learning an interesting game from another country," she said.

That gave David an idea. "What if we find out about games from other countries? We could use what we learn about games and **contests** to plan a World Games Day for our whole school," he suggested.

Ms. Gomez thought it was a great idea. The students began checking books out of the school library and searching Web sites on the Internet. They also talked to family members and neighbors who had lived in or visited other countries.

Soon the room was buzzing with talk about games and contests with interesting names such as "Throw the Beans," "Hopping House," and "Three Tins." The students gathered supplies, made posters about the rules, and planned how they would teach the games to the other classes. Now they were constantly talking about their plans for World Games Day.

When World Games Day finally arrived, everyone was very excited. Students from Ms. Gomez's class helped the other children learn how to play the games and compete in the contests. Soon everyone was having a wonderful time. All day long, children dashed from one game to the next. They didn't want to miss anything!

Near the end of the school day, Ms. Gomez came up to David. "Thank you!" she said.

"For what?" David asked, a little puzzled.

"You were the one who taught our class how to play broom hockey. You were also the one who had the idea for our World Games Day. We are all so glad you came to our school!"

"So am I!" answered David as he ran off to be with his new friends.

Cause and Effect

A *cause* is what makes something happen.
An *effect* is what happens.

▶ The boxes on the left each tell a cause. Write the effects in the boxes on the right. The first one has been done for you.

Cause

Effect

1. David was going to a new school, → so he was nervous. _____

2. Ken wanted David to feel welcome, → so Ken _____ _____.

3. David's classmates practiced basketball a lot, → _____ _____.

4. David wanted to fit in with the other kids, → _____ _____.

5. David played broom hockey more than basketball, → _____ _____.

Comprehension: Cause and Effect • Lesson 1   **13**

Comprehension

Cause and Effect

▶ Think about causes and effects in the story. Then fill in the missing causes and effects in the chart. The first one has been done for you.

Cause	Effect
The students wanted to learn to play broom hockey.	They asked David how to play.
_____	The students used the Internet to research games.
Ms. Gomez's class wanted to share new games.	_____
_____	Ms. Gomez thanked David.

14 Lesson 1 • Comprehension: Cause and Effect

Plural Nouns

A plural noun shows more than one.
Most words add *s* to show more than one.
book + *s* = books

book   books

When a word ends with a consonant + *y*, change the *y* to *i* and add *es* to show more than one.
stor*y* + *es* = stories

Some words are spelled differently to show more than one.
1 child/2 children   1 woman/2 women   1 man/2 men

▶ **Complete each sentence by writing the plural form of the word in parentheses.**

1. David and his _____ (friend) played broom hockey.
2. The students needed _____ (broom) for the game.
3. Their _____ (family) helped them find supplies.
4. They spent all of their _____ (Saturday) playing.
5. Then the _____ (child) decided to learn about games from other _____ (country).

▶ **Write about a topic your class might want to learn more about. Use the plural forms of two or more of the words in the box.**

| student | woman | man | family |

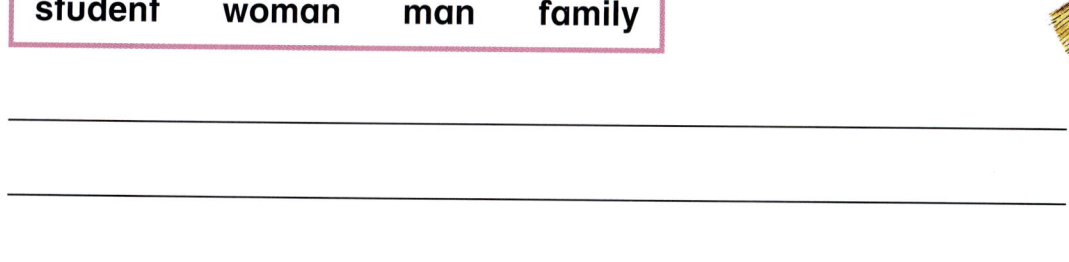

_____
_____
_____

Word Study: Plurals • Lesson 1 **15**

Vocabulary

Words to Learn

▶ Use the clues and the words from the box to complete the puzzle.

astonish	constantly	contest
dribble	encourage	hesitate
newcomer	puzzle	shoot

Clues

1. move a ball forward by bouncing it
2. gently push someone to do something
3. throw a ball toward a goal
4. to surprise
5. someone who has just come to a new place
6. pause because of feeling unsure
7. all the time
8. a game between two people or teams
9. to confuse

1. ___ ___ ___ B ___ ___
2. ___ ___ ___ ___ R ___ ___
3. ___ ___ O ___ ___
4. ___ ___ ___ O ___ ___ ___
5. ___ ___ ___ ___ M ___ ___
6. H ___ ___ ___ ___ ___ ___
7. O ___ ___ ___ ___ ___ ___ ___
8. C ___ ___ ___ ___ ___
   K E N
9. ___ ___ ___ ___ E
   P L A Y

16 Lesson 1 • Vocabulary

Reread

When you read, pay attention to the punctuation marks at the end of the sentences. Make your voice go up at the end of a sentence with a question mark. Make your voice sound excited when you see an exclamation point.

▶ Circle the question marks and exclamation points in the passage. Take turns reading aloud with a partner. Remember to use your voice to show expression.

When it was time for lunch, Ken invited David to sit with him and some other boys and girls in the lunchroom. After lunch, a girl named Lisa said, "We are crazy about basketball! We all play at recess and any other time we can. Do you want to play with us?"

David hesitated. He liked basketball, but he didn't play it very often. However, he wanted to fit in with his new friends. "Sure," David said, feeling a little nervous.

Recess seemed to go on for hours. David was amazed at the other students' skill. They could dribble the ball down the court as fast as lightning. They could shoot one basket after another without missing. David did his best, but he could see that he needed a lot more practice. The other children encouraged the newcomer to keep trying.

"Give yourself some time to learn," Lisa told him.
"You can do it, David," Ken said.

Writing

Extend and Write

▶ What game do you like to play? Write the name of the game in the chart and then list details such as the purpose of the game, what equipment is needed to play it, and how to play it.

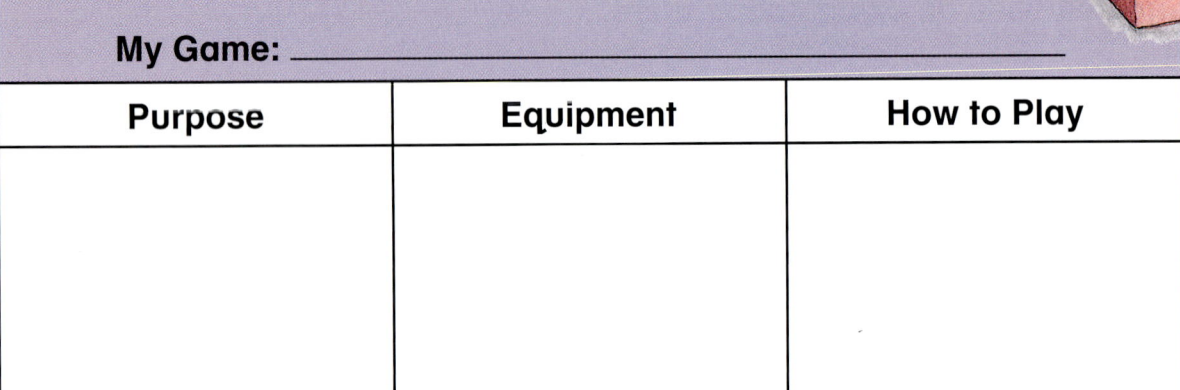

My Game: _____

Purpose	Equipment	How to Play

▶ Write an e-mail to explain your game to a friend.

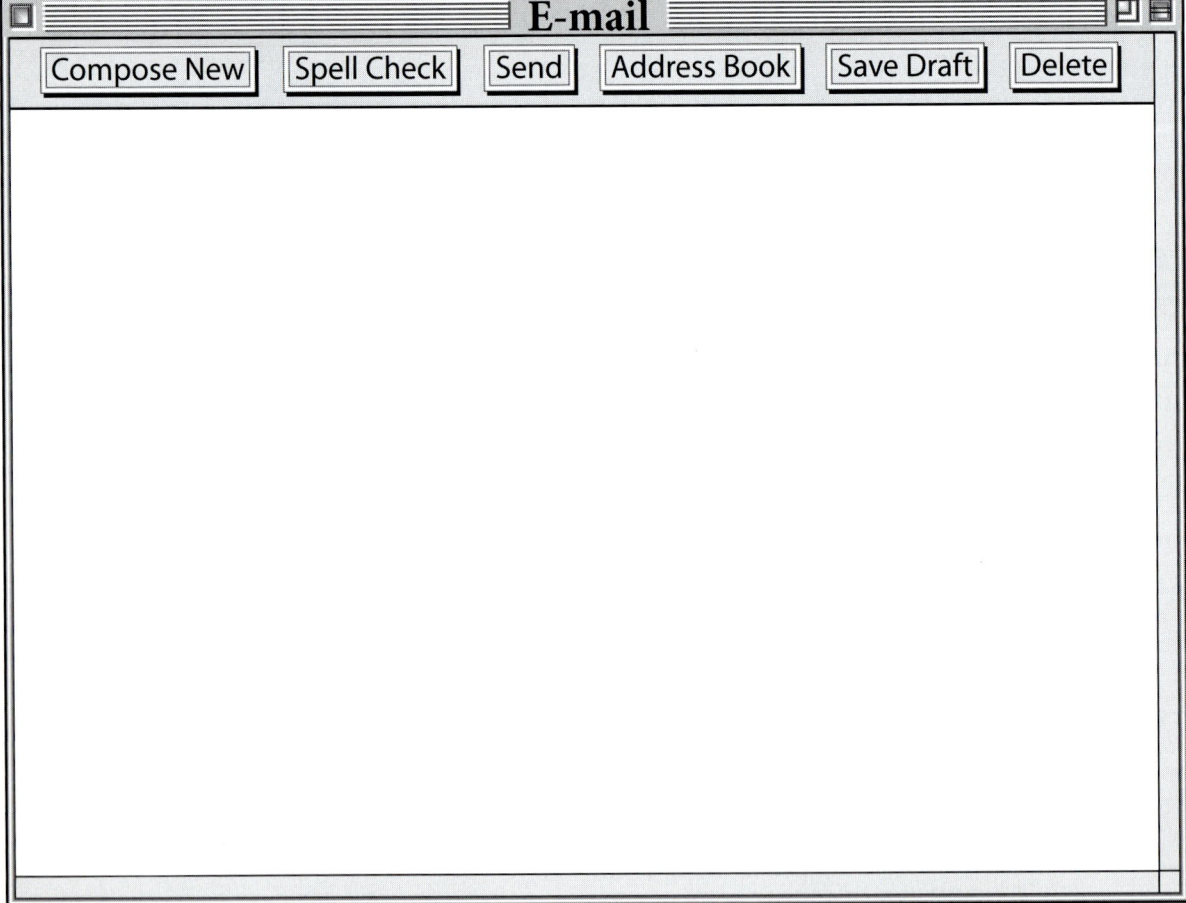

Get Ready to Read
Beetles Everywhere

1 Topic

beetles

2 Vocabulary

trait special feature of a person or other living thing

environment the setting where something lives

material what something is used for or made from

unique different from all others

scurry move quickly

fierce able to attack; dangerous

larva the wormlike form of a baby beetle

react do something because of what someone or something else does

3 Build Background

- What are some traits of beetles?
- Where do beetles live?

Lesson 2 19

Beetles Everywhere

A ladybug rests on a bush. Her bright, red wings decorated with black spots stand out on the green leaf. Ladybugs are just one kind of beetle. There are more than 250,000 other kinds of beetles! In fact, there are more kinds of beetles than there are kinds of plants on Earth.

Ladybug

Beetle Traits

Beetles are insects that come in all sizes. Some beetles are smaller than a dot made with a pencil. Others are as long as an adult's hand. Still, most beetles have some of the same **traits** as other beetles. For example, nearly all beetles have two sets of wings. They have soft wings for flying. These wings are covered by a hard set of wings for protection.

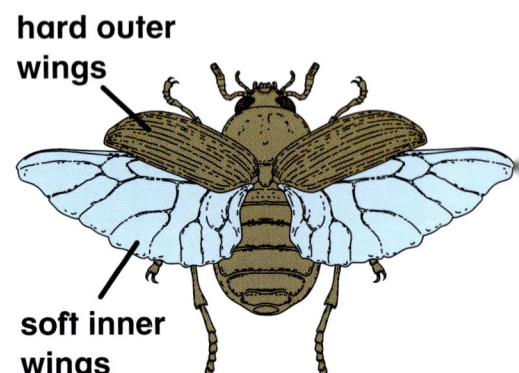

Beetles play an important role in the **environment.** They are helpful because they eat pests such as caterpillars. They also eat dead leaves and other **material** in the woods. However, beetles can cause trouble. They can destroy crops and spread sickness. These creatures have been on Earth since before dinosaurs. Why have beetles lasted so long? Maybe it is because of the **unique** ways they protect themselves.

Hercules beetle

Bombardier Beetles

The bombardier beetle got its name from what it does. In a way, it "drops a bomb." When another creature bothers it, two liquids mix together in a little pouch inside its body. Then the bombardier beetle shoots the liquid out of its body. The liquid comes out with a loud "pop" that scares the enemy. If the enemy does not move fast enough, it could get burned. The mixture is as hot as boiling water!

Bombardier beetle
(actual size about ½ inch long)

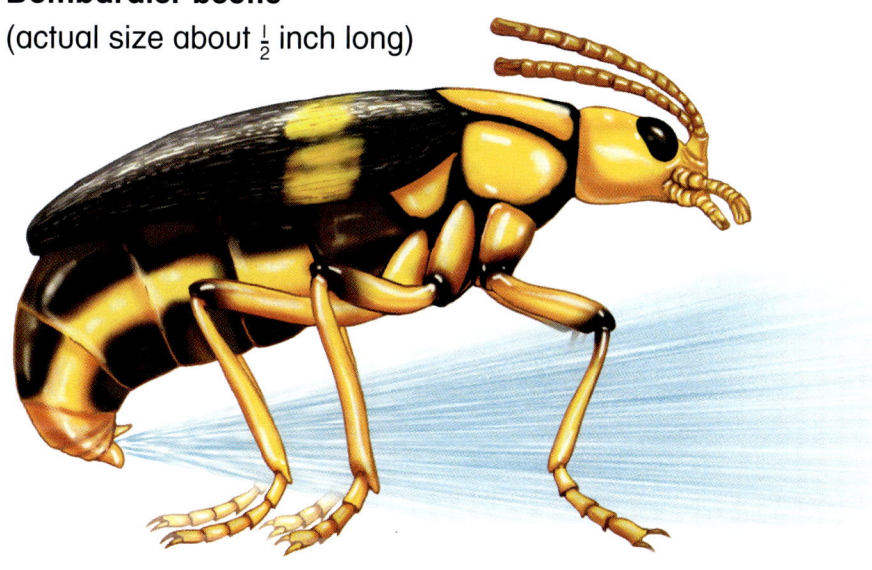

Click Beetles

Most click beetles are brown or black so that they match their environment. This coloring makes it hard for their enemies to find them.

When something does bother the click beetle, it uses sound to scare away its enemy. If another creature touches a click beetle, it falls on its back and plays dead. Then it rolls over and springs up with a loud click. This sound scares the enemy, which usually **scurries** away.

What trait makes it easy for click beetles to hide from their enemies?

Blister Beetles

Click beetles often match their environment to hide from their enemies, but blister beetles don't need to hide. They have another trick for protecting themselves. There is a poison in their bodies. It doesn't hurt blister beetles, but it can affect people and the animals that eat the beetles. Often people are hurt when a blister beetle lands on them and they try to brush it off. If a blister beetle is pressed or rubbed, its poison causes blisters.

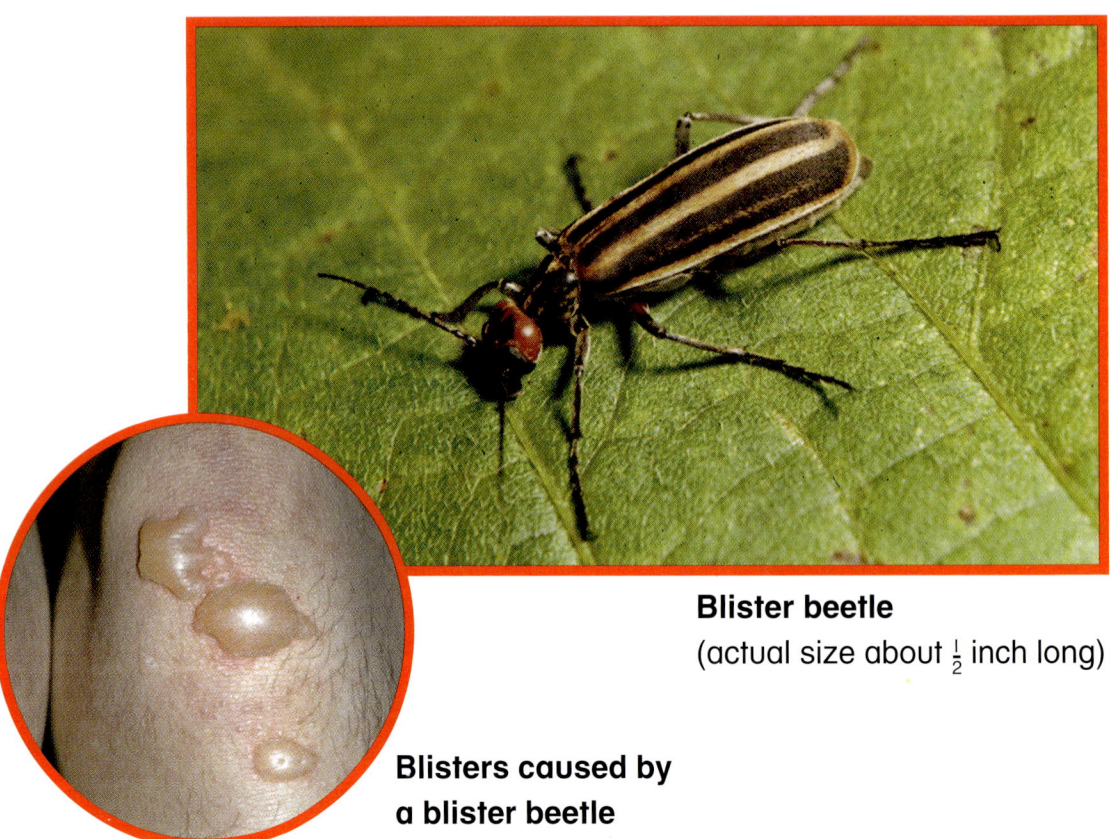

Blister beetle
(actual size about $\frac{1}{2}$ inch long)

Blisters caused by a blister beetle

You might be surprised at one use of blister beetle poison. Small doses of it can be mixed with other materials to make a medicine. Some doctors may use the medicine to treat warts.

Tiger beetle
(actual size ½ inch to 1 inch long)

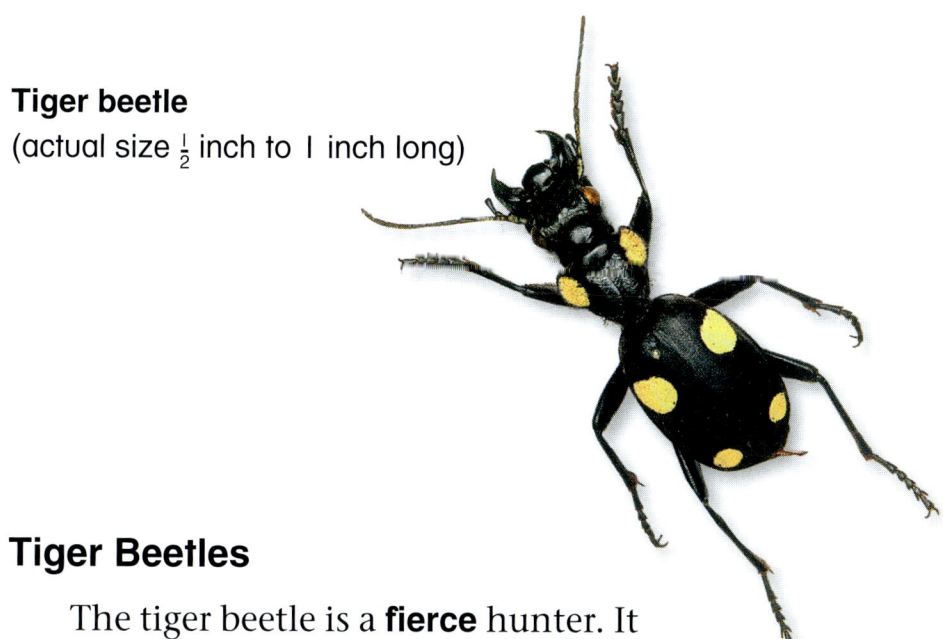

Tiger Beetles

The tiger beetle is a **fierce** hunter. It hunts down smaller insects and captures them with its sharp jaws. Even the **larva** of a tiger beetle is fierce! It doesn't go looking for food like the adult beetle does. It hides in a hole and waits until another insect passes by. Then it grabs the insect with its strong jaws. Hooks on the larva's stomach keep the other insect from pulling the larva out of its hole.

Different tiger beetles have different ways to **react** to enemies. Most tiger beetles can make a fast getaway in the air. African tiger beetles, however, cannot fly but are swift runners. Another trick that many tiger beetles use is sending out a bad smell if anything bothers them.

Rhinoceros Beetles

The rhinoceros beetle is named after another animal and shares a trait with that animal. Both rhinoceroses and rhinoceros beetles have horns.

> **Why do you think these beetles are called tiger beetles?**

Rhinoceros beetles use their horns to fight each other for food. They don't actually hurt the other beetles but use their horns to push and scare them away.

A close relative of the rhinoceros beetle is the Hercules beetle. These huge beetles can grow to be as big as seven inches long. Their horns may be as long as four inches.

Rhinoceros beetle (actual size about 1 inch to 2 $\frac{1}{2}$ inches long)

Tortoise Beetles

Tortoise beetles look something like a turtle, but they are only about as long as a grain of rice. These animals do not move around much. A tortoise beetle might spend its whole life on one leaf.

Tortoise beetles may not be good travelers, but they are smart parents. The mother tortoise beetle gathers her babies together and sits on them so that enemies will not see them. Sometimes a tortoise beetle larva slips out of its skin and makes the skin into a little umbrella-like shelter to protect itself.

Water Beetles

Water beetles live in ponds and lakes. These insects can fly, and they also swim with tiny paddle-like legs. One kind of water beetle is the whirligig beetle. A whirligig is a merry-go-round or a spinning toy. Whirligig beetles got their name because they spin around in groups on the water.

Water beetles' eyes are divided into two parts. One part is used above the water and the other part is used below the water. In this way, water beetles can see what is going on all around them. If something does sneak up on them, they react by giving off a bad-smelling, white liquid. Their enemies usually scurry away.

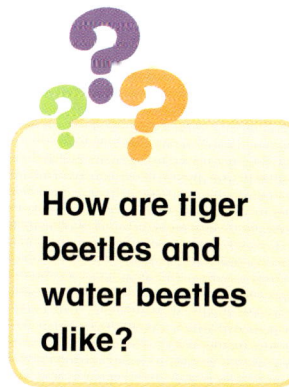

How are tiger beetles and water beetles alike?

Whirligig beetles
(actual size about $\frac{3}{4}$ inch long)

Beetles Forever!

Beetles come in many colors, sizes, and shapes and have unique ways to protect themselves. Some beetles make bad smells or surprising sounds, or drop "bombs" to scare away enemies. Others run, fly, swim, or hide from attackers. Helpful insects or pesky pests, beetles are interesting creatures.

Comprehension

Main Idea and Details

The main idea tells the most important idea in a paragraph or article. It tells what the paragraph or article is mostly about. Details tell more about the main idea.

▶ Read each passage below. For each passage, underline the main idea. Then list two details from the passage.

The bombardier beetle got its name from what it does. In a way, it "drops a bomb." When another creature bothers it, two liquids mix together in a little pouch inside its body. Then the bombardier beetle shoots the liquid out of its body. The liquid comes out with a loud "pop" that scares the enemy. If the enemy does not move fast enough, it could get burned. The mixture is as hot as boiling water!

Detail 1
_____
_____

Detail 2
_____
_____

The rhinoceros beetle is named after another animal and shares a trait with that animal. Both rhinoceroses and rhinoceros beetles have horns. Rhinoceros beetles use their horns to fight each other for food. They don't actually hurt the other beetles but use their horns to push and scare them away.

Detail 1
_____
_____

Detail 2
_____
_____

Main Idea and Details

▶ Read the main idea in the center box below. Add details to fill in the other boxes. The first one has been done for you.

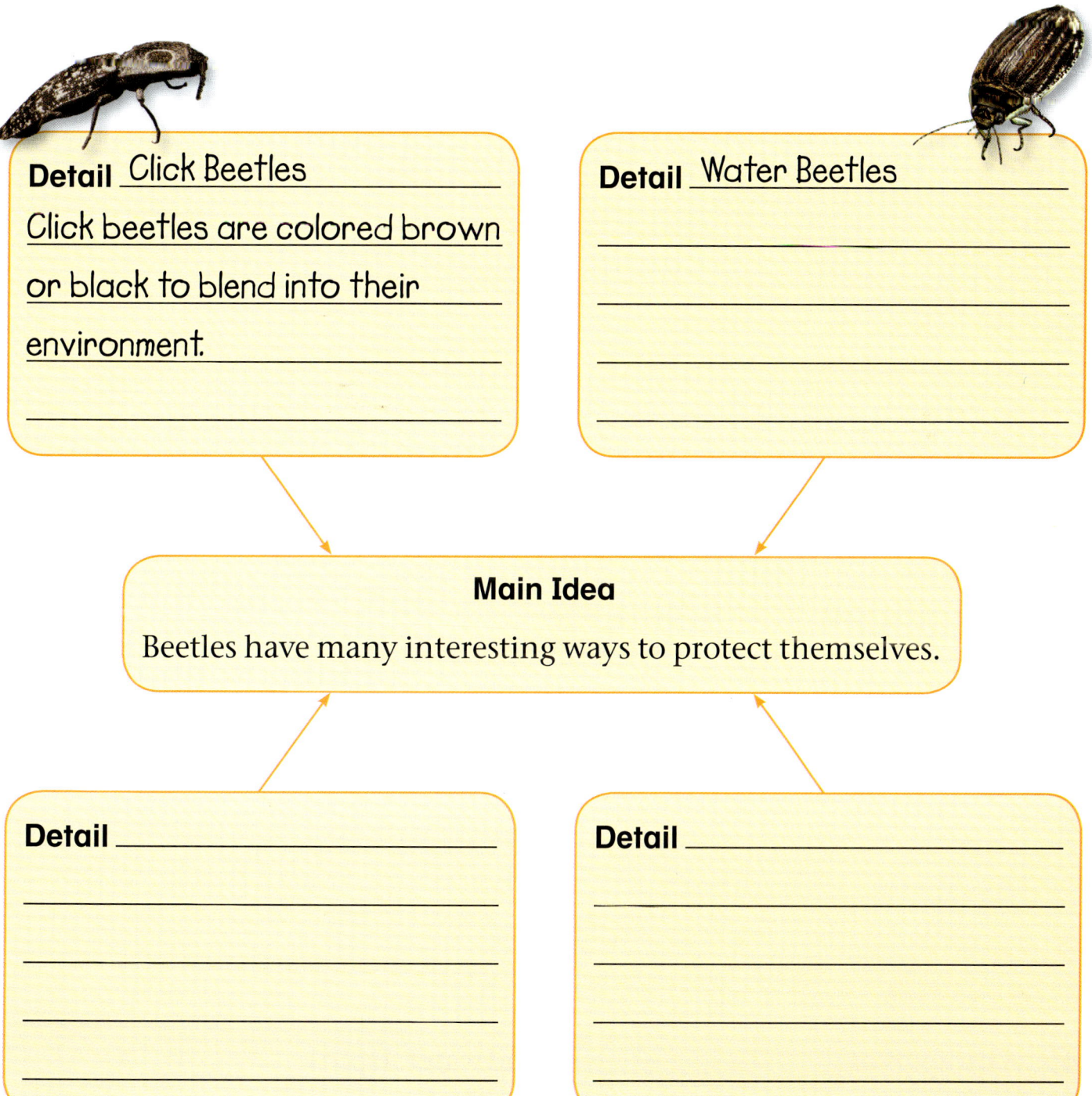

Detail **Click Beetles**
Click beetles are colored brown or black to blend into their environment.

Detail **Water Beetles**

Main Idea
Beetles have many interesting ways to protect themselves.

Detail

Detail

Word Study

Verb Endings: *s, ed,* and *ing*

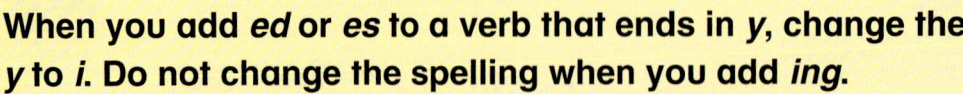

Verb endings help show when an action takes place. Follow these rules when you add endings to verbs.

Add *es* to verbs that end in *x*, *ch*, *sh*, *s*, or *z*.
mix + es = mixes   push + es = pushes

When you add *ed* or *es* to a verb that ends in *y*, change the *y* to *i*. Do not change the spelling when you add *ing*.
tr*y* + es = tries   tr*y* + ed = tried   try + ing = trying

When you add *ed* or *ing* to a word that ends in *e*, drop the *e*.
cur*e* + ing = curing

When you add *ed* or *ing* to a verb that ends in a vowel followed by a consonant, double the consonant before adding the ending.
rub + b + ed = rubbed

▶ **Read each sentence. Look at the word after each sentence. Add the ending *s*, *ed*, or *ing* to the word so it makes sense in the sentence. Write the word on the line.**

1 _____ special medicine with blister beetle poison may remove warts. (Use)

2 The tiger beetle _____ an insect with its jaws. (grab)

3 The insect _____ away when it heard the click beetle's sound. (scurry)

4 Whirligigs are _____ on the water. (spin)

5 A click beetle's color _____ its environment. (match)

28 Lesson 2 • Word Study: Verb Endings -*s*, -*ed*, -*ing*

Words to Learn

▶ Use the words in the box to match each word with its meaning.

environment	larva	material	trait

1. special feature of a person or thing _____
2. what is used to make something _____
3. the setting where something lives _____
4. the wormlike form of a baby beetle _____

▶ Choose the word in the box that completes each sentence below.

unique	scurry	react	fierce

Tiger beetles are as tough and _____ as the big cat with whom they share a name. Tiger beetles can also _____ to enemies by sending out a bad smell. Tiger beetles can _____ away from enemies, too. Are tiger beetles ordinary? Not at all! In fact, they are quite _____.

Vocabulary • Lesson 2

Fluency

Reread

> When you read aloud, try to read at the same speed you would when you talk. Practice difficult words before you read so that you can easily read them aloud.

▶ Reread the passage to yourself. Draw a line under any difficult words. Practice them until you can read each one easily. Then read the passage to a partner.

Tiger Beetles

The tiger beetle is a fierce hunter. It hunts down smaller insects and captures them with its sharp jaws. Even the larva of a tiger beetle is fierce! It doesn't go looking for food like the adult beetle does. It hides in a hole and waits until another insect passes by. Then it grabs the insect with its strong jaws. Hooks on the larva's stomach keep the other insect from pulling the larva out of its hole.

Different tiger beetles have different ways to react to enemies. Most tiger beetles can make a fast getaway in the air. African tiger beetles, however, cannot fly but are swift runners. Another trick that many tiger beetles use is sending out a bad smell if anything bothers them.

Extend and Write

▶ Choose one of the beetles you have read about. Pretend you are a scientist observing this beetle. List traits of the beetle in the idea web below. List how it sounds, looks, and protects itself.

How It Sounds

How It Looks

Name of beetle

How It Protects Itself

Other Traits

▶ Write a description of your beetle in the science log below.

3 Get Ready to Read
A Gift of Words

1 Characters

 **Luisa** a girl

 **Grandma Rosa** Luisa's grandmother

 **Mom** Luisa's mother

 **Dad** Luisa's father

2 Setting: Luisa's home

3 Vocabulary

fantastic very good, wonderful
anxious worried
memorize learn by heart
performance a play or a show
errand a short trip to do something
eager wanting to do something
grateful wanting to show thanks
amaze surprise very much

4 Build Background

- How could someone help you learn something new?
- What do you have to learn to be in a play?

A Gift of Words

Luisa ran home from school and rushed to the kitchen where Mom was baking a blueberry pie. "I have exciting news!" Luisa exclaimed with her eyes sparkling. "I'm going to be Dorothy in our school play, *The Wizard of Oz!* Mom, will you help me rehearse?"

"That's wonderful! Of course I'll help you, but I can't do it right now," Mom answered. "You know that Grandma Rosa arrives from Puerto Rico on Sunday, and I have to prepare for her to move in with us."

Luisa ran off calling, "Dad! Dad!" She found her father in the guest room making the bed.

When he heard Luisa's news, he said, "**Fantastic!** I'll be glad to help you rehearse, but not right now. I have to get Grandma's room ready. We want her to feel welcome."

Next, Luisa peeked into her brother Juan's room and found him frowning over a pile of textbooks and papers. He was happy about Luisa's news, too. "I know you'll do a great job," he said. "I'll help you rehearse, but not now. I have too much homework to do."

Luisa went out on the porch and looked at the script. "Wow, I have lines on every page," she thought, feeling a little **anxious**. "How will I ever **memorize** them?"

On Sunday, the family drove to the airport and waited for Grandma's plane. At last, they saw her in the crowd. "*¡Hola!*" she cried.

"Hello!" all four of them said at once and gathered around Grandma to hug her.

In the car, Grandma talked to Mom and Dad in Spanish. Luisa's parents had not spoken Spanish much since they moved from Puerto Rico. They had learned English before Luisa was born, but they still remembered enough Spanish to talk with Grandma. Luisa didn't understand the language, but she could tell from Grandma's voice that she was glad to be with them.

How might things change when Grandma moves in with the family?

Luisa loved having Grandma Rosa live with them. She loved Grandma's cheerful laughter that carried all over the house. She loved hearing her speak Spanish, even though Luisa didn't understand the words. She also loved the tasty foods Grandma cooked. Her favorites were *flan*, a sweet, soft pudding, and fried plantains, which were like bananas. Luisa was having lots of fun, but she wasn't learning her lines for the play. She began to worry whether she would be ready for the **performance.**

When Luisa came to breakfast on Saturday morning, her family was already seated around the table. They were enjoying the breakfast that Grandma had made. Luisa breathed in the delicious coffee smell of her parents' *café con leche,* a special coffee with milk. She piled some of Grandma's fluffy pancakes on her plate and spooned some juicy mango fruit on the top. Then she asked, "Can someone please help me practice today?"

"I have a lot of **errands** to run today, but maybe I can help tomorrow," said Mom.

"I promised my friend Mike that I would help him work on his car, and I am afraid it will take all day," said Dad.

"I wish I could help, but I have a softball game to play," said Juan.

"*Yo,*" Grandma said, pointing to herself.

Luisa looked surprised. How could Grandma help? She did not know English, but she looked so **eager.** Luisa really needed to practice, too, so she smiled and nodded "yes" to Grandma.

After everyone left, Grandma and Luisa sat at the kitchen table, and Luisa read her lines. It helped to say them out loud. Hearing her own voice reminded Luisa to read with feeling. Grandma smiled and clapped. Luisa felt good about herself, and she was **grateful** that Grandma Rosa wanted to help.

Luisa's parents and brother always seemed to be busy with errands or sports, so she was grateful that Grandma had lots of time for her. Every day, she listened to her granddaughter rehearse her lines and watched her act out her part. Soon, Luisa had memorized the script. One day, Grandma **amazed** Luisa by saying, "Good job!"

"You speak English!" Luisa exclaimed.

"*Un poco,*" said Grandma.

"Yes, a little," replied Luisa. She suddenly realized that she had learned some Spanish and Grandma Rosa had learned some English. They were starting to understand each other as they worked together.

After weeks of practice, the important day arrived. The family drove to Luisa's school, eager to see the play. Grandma gave Luisa a hug, and Luisa was the only one who heard her whisper, "You will be great!"

Luisa thanked Grandma and rushed off to get ready. She did not feel anxious anymore, because she knew she could do well.

Why was Luisa so sure she could do well?

Luisa did. In fact, all the actors did a fantastic job. Everyone clapped loudly at the end of the performance. When the actors came back on stage to take a bow, the principal gave each performer a bunch of flowers just like real actors receive after a show. Luisa smiled as she took her flowers. Then she amazed everyone. She went down the stage steps and walked toward Grandma. She didn't care that everyone got quiet. She didn't care that they were all staring at her. She had something important to do. Luisa walked up to Grandma and gave her the flowers. "*Gracias,*" Luisa said to her grandmother. "Thank you!"

Smiling her biggest smile, Grandma answered loudly enough for everyone to hear. "You're welcome!"

Understanding Characters

Characters are the people or animals in a story. You can learn about the characters by noticing what they say, do, think, and feel.

▶ Read the clues in the chart below. Fill in the empty boxes to tell about the characters.

What the Character Says or Does	Character
"I have to get Grandma's room ready."	Dad
"You will be great."	
She gave Grandma flowers.	
	Mom

▶ Write one thing that Luisa says or does. Then tell what this shows about Luisa.

_____
_____
_____
_____
_____
_____

Comprehension

Understanding Characters

When you read a story, watch for words that tell you what the character says, feels, or thinks. Sometimes a character changes throughout the story. List ways that Luisa and Grandma Rosa change over time.

How Characters Changed

Luisa is anxious about learning her lines.	Grandma Rosa does not know English.
Luisa practices her lines with Grandma Rosa.	Grandma Rosa offers to help Luisa practice.
_____ _____ _____ _____	_____ _____ _____ _____
Luisa is proud of how she does in the play.	Grandma Rosa speaks English in public.

Word Study

Words with More Than One Meaning

Some words have more than one meaning. Which meaning of right is used in this sentence?

Mom knew the right way to make a pie.
- opposite of left
- correct

▶ **Read each sentence. Look at the underlined word. Put an X in the box next to the correct meaning of the word in the sentence.**

1 Luisa had to learn her part in the show.
- ☐ let someone see
- ☐ play

2 Mom, Dad, and Juan had lots to do.
- ☐ much
- ☐ pieces of land

3 They left the house.
- ☐ opposite of right
- ☐ went away from

▶ **Read the word and one of its meanings. Write a sentence using the word with that meaning.**

1 **lots** (pieces of land)

_____

2 **left** (opposite of right)

_____

3 **show** (let someone see)

_____

Word Study: Words with Multiple Meanings • Lesson 3

Vocabulary

Words to Learn

▶ Write the correct word to finish each sentence.

1. Luisa needs to _____ (amaze/memorize) her part in the play.

2. She is _____ (eager/anxious) because she does not know if she can learn all her lines.

3. Luisa does a _____ (fantastic/grateful) job of learning her lines.

4. She is very happy with her _____ (errand/performance).

▶ Write about something you do well. Tell how you learned to do it and how you feel about doing it. Use at least three words from the box.

| fantastic | anxious | memorize | performance |
| errand | eager | grateful | amaze |

_____
_____
_____
_____
_____
_____
_____

Reread

> Quotation marks in a story show the words a character says. Think about how the character is feeling when he or she says those words. Make sure to read the character's words to show those feelings.

▶ Underline what each character says in the passage below. Then take turns reading aloud the parts of Luisa, Mom, Dad, Juan, and Grandma with a partner. Change your voice to fit what each character says.

    Luisa piled some of Grandma's fluffy pancakes on her plate and spooned some juicy mango fruit on the top. Then she asked, "Can someone please help me practice today?"
    "I have a lot of errands to run today, but maybe I can help tomorrow," said Mom.
    "I promised my friend Mike that I would help him work on his car, and I am afraid it will take all day," said Dad.
    "I wish I could help, but I have a softball game to play," said Juan.
    "*Yo*," Grandma said, pointing to herself.
    Luisa looked surprised. How could Grandma help? She did not know English, but she looked so eager. Luisa really needed to practice, too, so she smiled and nodded "yes" to Grandma.

Fluency

Fluency • Lesson 3

Writing

Extend and Write

In the story, Luisa helped Grandma Rosa learn English while Grandma Rosa helped Luisa learn her lines for the play. What if Luisa decided to teach something to a friend? Use a word web to list things that Luisa is interested in or does well.

▶ Choose one idea from your word web. Write a story about Luisa teaching something to a friend.

Get Ready to Read
Tsunamis: Danger from the Sea

1 Topic

tsunamis

2 Vocabulary

series a group of similar things coming one after another

earthquake a very hard shaking of the ground

vibration a shaking or moving back and forth

dangerous causing harm

gigantic huge; very large

damage loss or harm

crumble break into small pieces

survivor person who stays alive after a harmful event

predict tell what is going to happen later

expand make bigger

3 Build Background

- What causes ocean waves?
- How does an ocean wave look, feel, and sound?

Tsunamis: Danger from the Sea

Most waves splash on the shore and go quietly back to sea, but some waves are much larger. They smash buildings, pull trees out by their roots, and wash away cars, trucks, and even homes as if they were toys. This kind of wave is called a *tsunami* (tsoo-NAH-mee).

What is a tsunami?

A tsunami is a **series** of very large ocean waves. The word *tsunami* comes from a Japanese word that means "harbor wave." Over the years, tsunamis have destroyed Japanese communities built next to harbors. Tsunamis are also called *tidal waves,* but tides do not cause them.

What causes a tsunami?

If tides do not cause tsunamis, what does? In most cases, **earthquakes** under the ocean floor cause these huge waves. During an earthquake, part of the Earth shakes very hard. These **vibrations** of the Earth send out waves in all directions, like ripples that go out when a rock is thrown into a pond.

How waves build

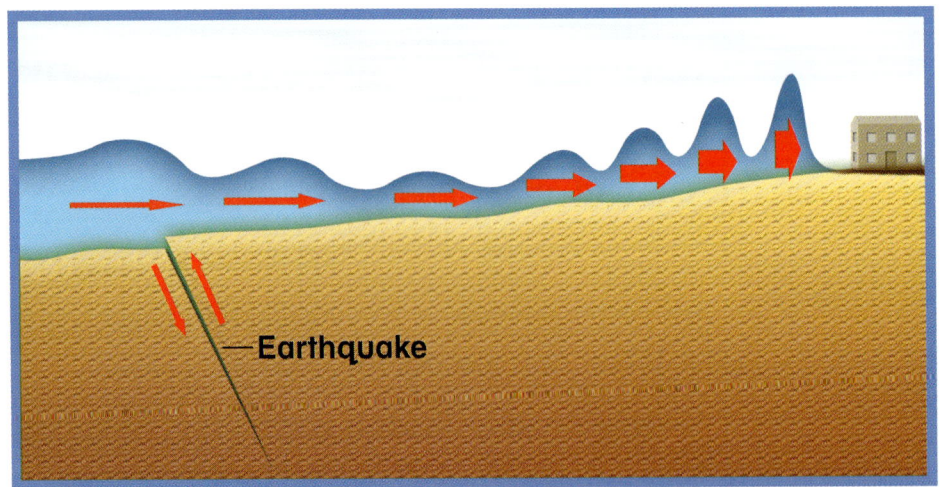

How are tsunami waves different from other waves?

On a very windy day, waves caused by wind can be as high as ten feet. A **dangerous** hurricane with strong winds can make waves more than 45 feet high.

Tsunami waves are much higher than wind waves. They are **gigantic,** reaching as high as 100 feet, or as tall as an eight-story building.

Unlike wind waves, which usually come to shore about ten seconds apart, tsunami waves may arrive up to an hour apart. Does this mean that tsunami waves are slower? No, they are just farther apart. Far out in the ocean, wind waves average about 500 feet apart, a little longer than one-and-a-half football fields. Tsunami waves can be more than 60 miles apart, about as far as you could travel in a car on the highway in an hour!

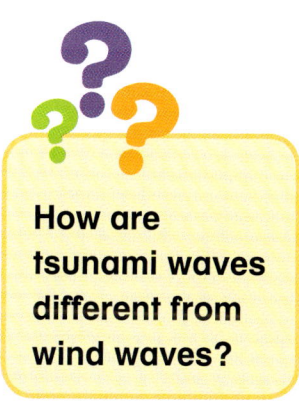

How are tsunami waves different from wind waves?

Comparison of wind wave to tsunami wave

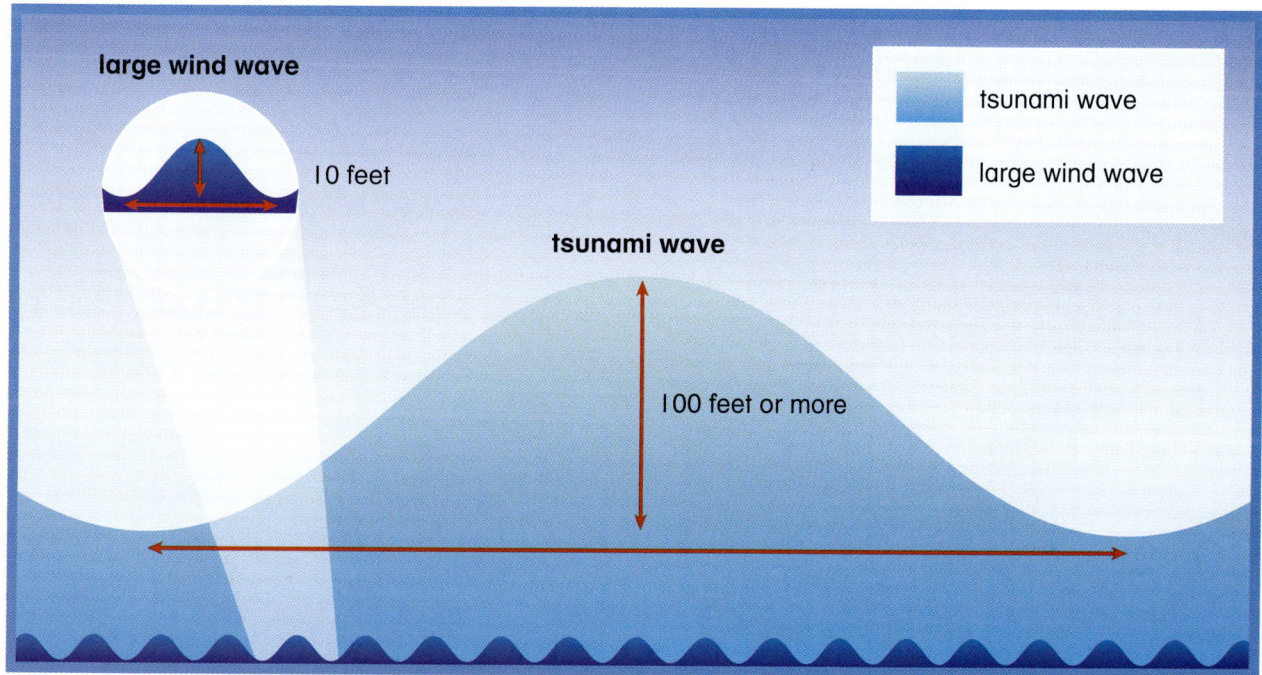

What effect do tsunami waves have?

Sometimes tsunamis have little effect. In the middle of the ocean, a ship can sail over tsunami waves and not even know it. A plane can fly over a tsunami, and a passenger looking out the window will not even see it.

At other times, tsunamis are the most dangerous of all waves. Both their size and their speed make tsunamis dangerous. Right after an earthquake, when tsunami waves are in the middle of the ocean, they may travel 600 miles an hour, as fast as a jet plane. These waves can cross the whole Pacific Ocean in a day. By the time they reach the shore, they "slow down" to 100 miles an hour. When a tsunami hits land, it is as if an eight-story building going twice as fast as a car slams into the land. These gigantic walls of water destroy everything they hit.

Tsunami damage in Indonesia in 2004

These enormous waves cause horrible **damage.** They wash away buildings, roads, and bridges. They pull up trees, kill animals and plants, and change the shape of the land. Many people lose their lives in a tsunami. Because tsunamis are a series of waves, the danger can continue for several hours. Even bigger waves can follow the first one.

A terrible tsunami happened in 1960. It was caused by the strongest earthquake that had ever been recorded. First, the tsunami hit Chile in South America. It also raced across the Pacific Ocean for fourteen hours until it smashed into Hawaii. Eight hours later, it crashed into Japan. The tsunami **crumbled** steel and concrete buildings as if they were sand castles. The waves caused millions of dollars in damage. About 2,000 people lost their lives. For three more days, smaller waves bounced across the ocean.

What kind of damage can a tsunami cause?

1960 tsunami travel times

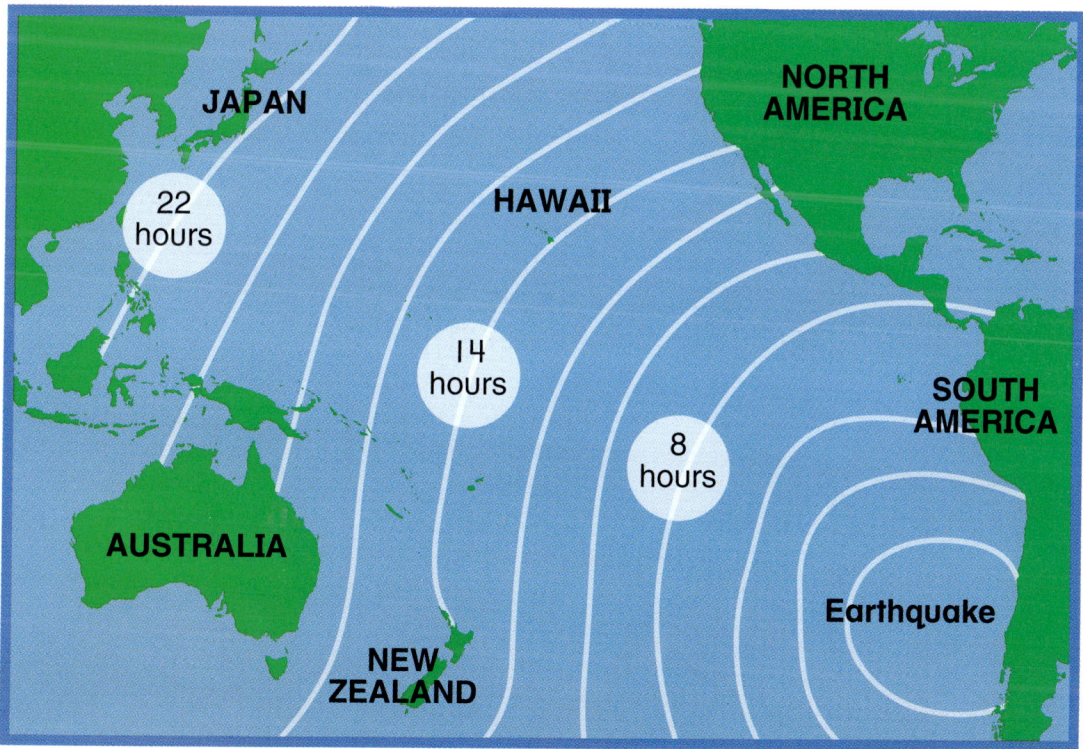

In 2004, one of the world's worst tsunamis hit some Asian countries. More than 125,000 people died. One **survivor** said, "It was like being in a blender."

How do people protect themselves from tsunamis?

When a tsunami is coming toward land, people need to get to higher ground quickly. In 2004, the people on one island in Asia remembered a warning that saved their lives. Their grandparents had said to "head for the hills" if the Earth ever started to shake.

Because a tsunami moves very fast, early warning helps save lives. The more time people have to get out of the deadly path, the more survivors there are. Scientists have found ways to **predict** tsunamis and warn people.

After a tsunami in 1946, a warning system was set up in Hawaii. The system picks up vibrations of earthquakes under the sea. Scientists figure out where a tsunami is likely to hit, and they send out a warning.

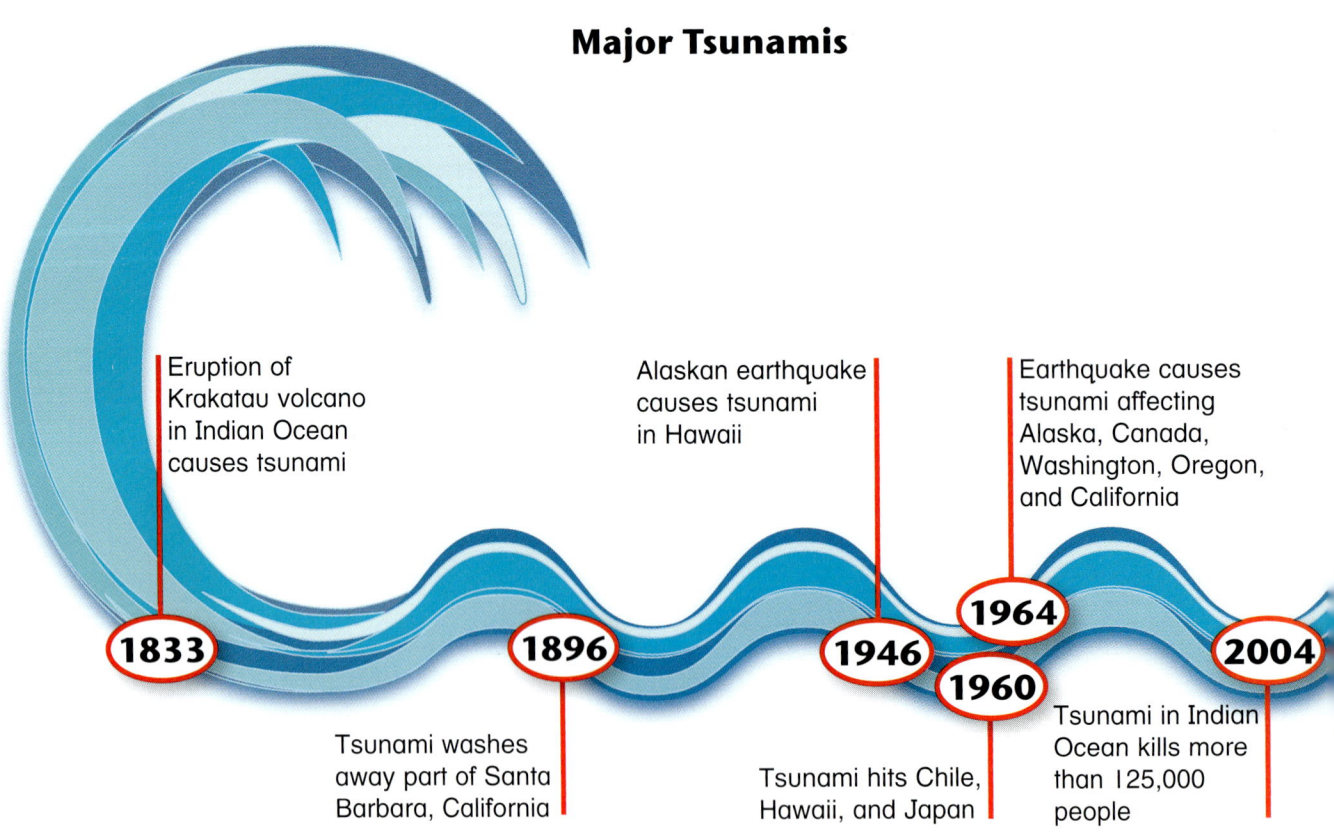

Major Tsunamis

- **1833** Eruption of Krakatau volcano in Indian Ocean causes tsunami
- **1896** Tsunami washes away part of Santa Barbara, California
- **1946** Alaskan earthquake causes tsunami in Hawaii
- **1960** Tsunami hits Chile, Hawaii, and Japan
- **1964** Earthquake causes tsunami affecting Alaska, Canada, Washington, Oregon, and California
- **2004** Tsunami in Indian Ocean kills more than 125,000 people

After tsunamis in the Pacific Ocean in the 1960s, the United States helped **expand** the warning system. Scientists from 26 countries use the bigger system to look for earthquakes that could cause tsunamis anywhere in the Pacific Ocean. Because eight out of ten tsunamis happen in the Pacific Ocean, the system helps protect people.

This system is for the Pacific Ocean, so it did not warn people of the horrible tsunami in the Indian Ocean in 2004. Now countries are exploring how to expand the system even more so it can warn people about these dangerous waves anywhere in the world.

Tsunamis are the most powerful waves on Earth. They destroy wildlife, crumble cities, and hurt and kill people. Scientists are working hard to learn more about these killer waves. This will help them predict tsunamis earlier and prevent so many lost lives.

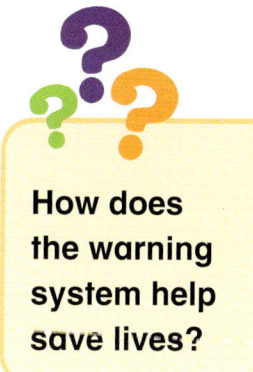

How does the warning system help save lives?

June 23, 2004

December 28, 2004

Serious damage to Indonesian city by the 2004 tsunami

Comprehension

Comparing and Contrasting

Comparing is finding ways that things are alike. Contrasting is finding ways that things are different. Sometimes authors use clue words such as *like* or *same* to compare. They may use words such as *different* or *unlike* to contrast, or they may use words ending in *er* or *est*, such as *brighter* and *brightest*.

▶ Circle the two things in each sentence that are being compared or contrasted. Tell how they are alike or different.

1. Unlike wind waves, which usually come to shore about ten seconds apart, tsunami waves may arrive up to an hour apart.

   _____

   _____

2. When tsunami waves are in the middle of the ocean, they may travel 600 miles an hour, as fast as a jet plane.

   _____

   _____

3. Tsunami waves are much higher than wind waves.

   _____

   _____

Comprehension

Comparing and Contrasting

▶ Think about how wind waves and tsunamis are different from each other. Write words in each box to contrast the two types of waves. Look back at the article to check the facts.

Details	Wind Waves	Tsunami Waves
1 Cause		
2 Height		
3 Distance apart		
4 Time between waves		
5 Dangers		

Word Study

Adjectives That Compare

You can use adjectives to compare things. To compare two things, use adjectives with *er* at the end. To compare more than two things, use adjectives with *est* at the end.

When you add *er* or *est* to a word that ends in *e*, drop the *e*.

large   larger   largest

When you add *er* or *est* to a word that ends with a consonant + *y*, change the *y* to *i*. Then add the ending.

scary   scarier   scariest

When you add *er* or *est* to a word that ends in a vowel followed by a consonant, double the consonant.

hot   hotter   hottest

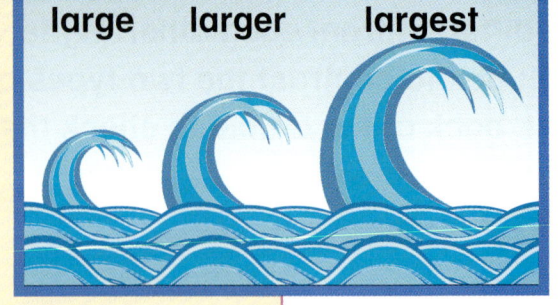

large   larger   largest

▶ Complete each sentence by adding *er* or *est* to the word in parentheses so it makes sense in the sentence.

1 Tsunami waves are the _____ of all waves. (high)

2 Are wind waves or tsunami waves _____? (slow)

3 Tsunami waves travel _____ out in the ocean than they do near the shore. (fast)

4 When tsunami waves come close to shore, they get _____. (big)

5 The 2004 tsunami was one of the _____ ever to hit land. (large)

6 Scientists want to warn people about tsunamis _____ than they have in the past. (early)

54   Lesson 4 • Word Study: Adjectives That Compare

Words to Learn

▶ Read the clues below. Find a word in the word box to answer each clue and use your answers to complete the puzzle.

| crumble | damage | dangerous | earthquake | expand |
| gigantic | predict | series | survivor | vibration |

Across

5. huge, very large
7. loss or harm
8. a very hard shaking of the ground
9. person who stays alive after a harmful event
10. break into small pieces

Down

1. a group of similar things coming one after another
2. make bigger
3. a shaking or moving back and forth
4. tell what is going to happen later
6. harmful

Vocabulary

Fluency

Reread

> It is important to read nonfiction carefully to make sure you understand the information correctly. Before you read, review the passage to make sure you know what each word means and how it is pronounced.

▶ **Practice any difficult words before reading. Then read aloud to a partner.**

On a very windy day, waves caused by wind can be as high as ten feet. A dangerous hurricane with strong winds can make waves more than 45 feet high.

Tsunami waves are much higher than wind waves. They are gigantic, reaching as high as 100 feet, or as tall as an eight-story building.

Wind waves usually come to shore about ten seconds apart, but tsunami waves may arrive up to an hour apart. Does this mean that tsunami waves are slower? No, they are just farther apart. Far out in the ocean, wind waves average about 500 feet apart, a little longer than one-and-a-half football fields. Tsunami waves can be more than 60 miles apart, about as far as you could travel in a car on the highway in an hour!

Writing

Extend and Write

▶ Some students in your school have heard about tsunamis in the news, but they are confused about what tsunamis are. You decide to write an article comparing and contrasting tsunami waves and wind waves for the school paper. Use the Venn diagram to list facts about the two kinds of waves to use in your article. Then write the article.

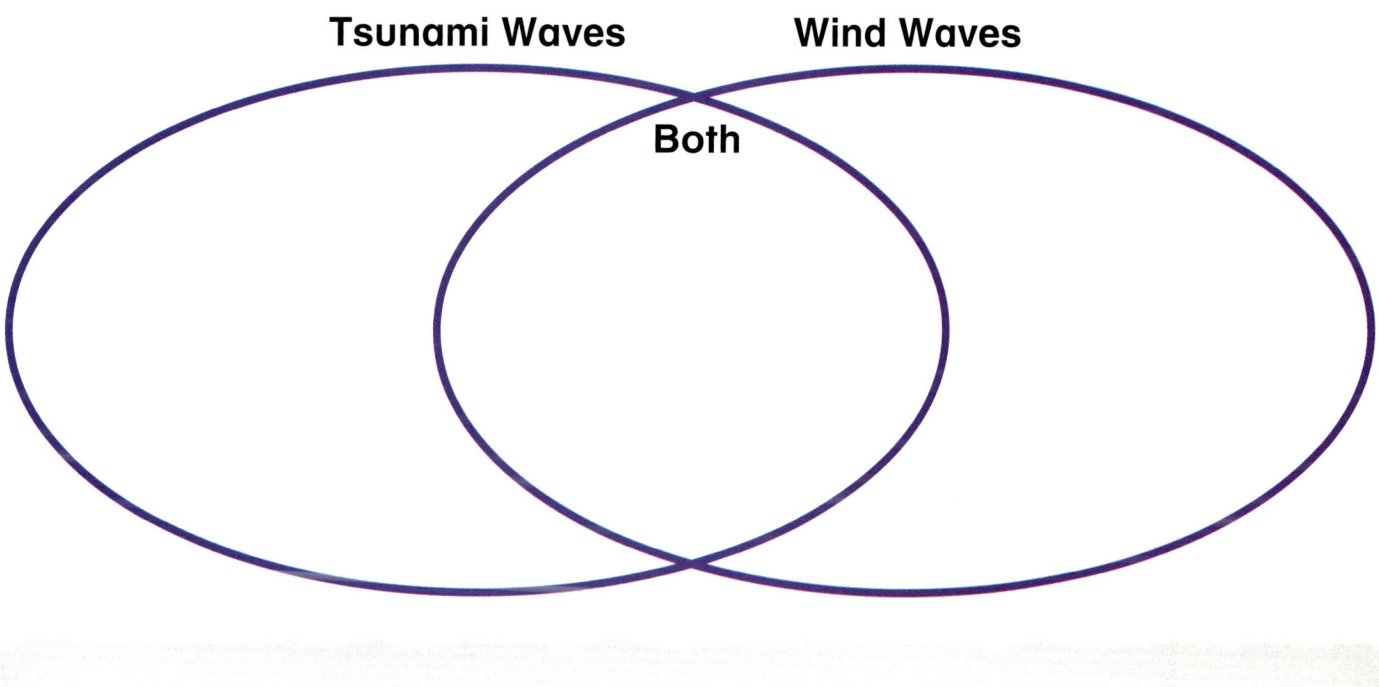

5

Get Ready to Read

John Hockenberry: Reporting on the World

1 Topic

journalist John Hockenberry

2 Vocabulary

journalist person who tells the news

correspondent journalist who travels to report a story

diverse different

career person's job or series of jobs through life

paralyzed not able to move

microphone device used to send a voice to another place

produce plan and write a show

edit make spoken or written words more clear

refugee person who must leave home because of a war

3 Build Background

- What do you know about a news reporter's job?
- What skills would you need to be a news reporter?

John Hockenberry: Reporting on the World

You may have seen this man on TV at home. He is John Hockenberry, a **journalist**. John gives news reports on a nighttime TV news program, and he talks to all kinds of interesting people. John also travels all over the world as a news **correspondent**. Every day John's job is a little different, and he says he likes that just fine. "I have a lot of **diverse** interests," says John.

A Boy with Many Interests

Even when John was a boy in school, he had many interests. He liked math, and he really liked music. Besides listening to music, John played the guitar and piano. Because he was so interested in all people, John had friends of all ages.

John didn't know what he would be when he grew up. What **career** would let him explore all his interests? The road to John's future would have many twists and turns that he could never have imagined.

John Hockenberry in Somalia, 1993

A Day That Changed Everything

John's life changed forever on a day in 1976 that started like any other day. John was 19 years old and was studying math at the University of Chicago. He and his roommate got a ride to travel to Massachusetts with two other students.

During the trip, the car ran off the road and crashed down a hill. The accident killed the car's driver. One of the other passengers was hurt, but not too much. John's spinal cord was torn, and his lower body was **paralyzed**. John Hockenberry would never be able to walk again.

On that day, John learned how easily a life can change completely. He also faced some tough questions. What would his life be like from now on? What would he do? John did not have a clear plan before he got hurt. Now that he was paralyzed, the future seemed even more uncertain. John had always been creative, though, and he was ready to face the future.

John when he was in high school, 1974

John still loved music. A few years after the accident, he went back to college to study music. This time, he chose the University of Oregon. John's life in a wheelchair was very different, but he made friends and enjoyed his new life in Oregon.

A Voice on the Air

One day in 1980, John heard of an unpaid job reading the news at the local public radio station. He went there and read a story into the **microphone.** When John heard his voice on the air, he was thrilled! He knew this was what he wanted to do with his life.

John's boss liked John's work. He said John could **produce** his own programs, "as long as you get your facts right."

John said that he learned a lot by hearing "some of my best ideas and some of my worst ideas" on the air. One important lesson he learned was how to **edit** his ideas while speaking. Thinking through what you mean to say before you say it is a necessary skill if you're the voice behind the microphone!

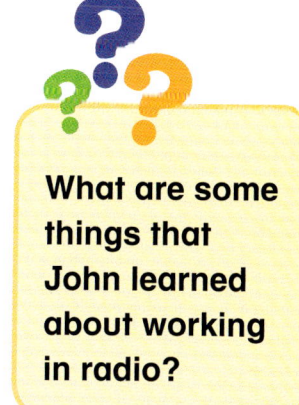

What are some things that John learned about working in radio?

John Hockenberry, young radio announcer

Traveling for the Story

Later that year, John got a chance to become a news reporter. This was very exciting, but John was worried. Would he be able to get around well enough to follow a story? John fixed his wheelchair with special parts. Sometimes he would have to be in places with rough roads or no sidewalks. John used special tires and made steel plates that protected the wheel gears. He learned to be ready for anything.

John soon had a job as a news correspondent for National Public Radio. This job included traveling to the Middle East and interviewing leaders of countries, but John also talked with ordinary people. He felt it was part of his job to let his audience hear those voices.

In 1991, John was covering the Gulf War in Iraq. He wanted to interview Kurdish **refugees.** The people were leaving their homeland. There were no roads up to their camp, so John got a donkey. He tied himself on and headed into the mountains. Once at the camp, John talked to the refugees. He let them tell their sad stories. Then he shared those stories with the world.

Kurdish refugee camp, 1991

John Hockenberry watching girls playing in Albania

A New Assignment

In 1993, John Hockenberry got a new job doing stories for a nighttime TV news show. It was his first time working on television. Now people could see John when he talked. The news show had a huge audience. Millions of people would hear what he had to say about different topics.

John has become more than a reporter. He also comments on the news to help give people a better understanding of what it means. His interviews still include ones with world leaders as well as ordinary people. He always tries to choose stories that have meaning and to let people know his point of view.

Working on TV gives John a chance to explore the many things he enjoys. His interest in music and other cultures often shows up in his interviews. John has hosted two shows of his own. On one of these shows, called *Hockenberry,* John interviewed musicians, writers, and artists. His guests often performed or read from their work on the show. The show gave John a chance to offer diverse ideas to his audience.

Why was it important for John to interview so many different people?

63

Moving in Many Worlds

Today, John Hockenberry works on many projects. He is still a journalist on radio and TV. He was the host of a radio series about science and health, which he helped write.

John has also written two books. One book tells his life story. The other book is a mystery novel.

Theater audiences enjoyed a one-man show that John wrote and performed on the stage. The show, called *Spokesman,* told about John's life in a wheelchair.

John is very busy with all these projects, but his family is also important to him. One of his greatest pleasures is spending time with his wife and two sets of twins!

Fans of John Hockenberry's work always enjoy hearing what he has to say. They know that he will always be honest with his thoughts. They also love John's humor.

John would probably be the first to say that he has had a great career. He has found ways to share his thoughts with millions of people. Many years ago, John's injury changed the way he looked at life. Now he tries to give other people a fresh view on their world.

John Hockenberry and his family

Fact and Opinion

> It is important to know whether you are reading facts or opinions. A fact is something that you can prove is true. An opinion is what someone thinks, feels, or believes.

▶ Read these passages from the article. For each passage, write F if it is a fact and O if it is an opinion.

1. _____ John's spinal cord was torn, and his lower body was paralyzed.

2. _____ One day in 1980, John heard of a volunteer job reading the news at the local public radio station. He went there and read a story into the microphone.

3. _____ Fans of John Hockenberry's work always enjoy hearing what he has to say. They know that he will always be honest with his thoughts. They also love John's humor.

4. _____ John also travels all over the world as a news correspondent.

5. _____ John would probably be the first to say that he has had a great career.

Comprehension

Fact and Opinion

▶ Read the paragraph below. Then list two facts about the Hockenberrys in the Facts column. Write two of their opinions in the Opinions column.

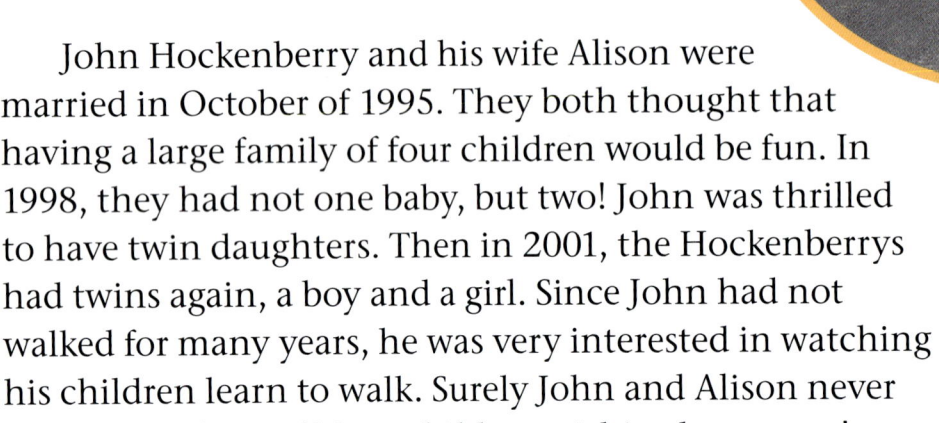

John Hockenberry and his wife Alison were married in October of 1995. They both thought that having a large family of four children would be fun. In 1998, they had not one baby, but two! John was thrilled to have twin daughters. Then in 2001, the Hockenberrys had twins again, a boy and a girl. Since John had not walked for many years, he was very interested in watching his children learn to walk. Surely John and Alison never expected to have all four children within three years!

Facts	Opinions
1	1
2	2

Word Study

Synonyms and Antonyms

Synonyms are words with the same or almost the same meanings. Antonyms are words with opposite meanings.

The word *strong* is a synonym for *powerful*.

The word *whisper* is an antonym for *shout*.

Read each sentence. Underline the word choice that is a synonym for the word in bold type. Draw an X through the antonym. Then rewrite the sentence using the synonym.

1. John was **thrilled** to hear his voice on the air!
   surprised   delighted   disappointed
   _____

2. The Kurdish people **fled** from their homes.
   escaped   stayed   called
   _____

3. The news show had an **enormous** audience.
   tiny   ordinary   huge
   _____

4. John offers a **fresh** view of the world.
   easy   familiar   new
   _____
   _____

Word Study: Synonyms and Antonyms • Lesson 5

Vocabulary

Words to Learn

▶ **Read each sentence. Choose the correct word from the two word choices.**

1. John Hockenberry feels very comfortable speaking into a _____ (microphone/career).

2. As a _____ (journalist/refugee), he tries to give the audience the facts.

3. It is fun to hear John's thoughts about many _____ (paralyzed/diverse) topics.

4. To state his ideas well, he had to learn to _____ (edit/produce) his work.

5. John often works with others to _____ (diverse/produce) new programs.

6. John Hockenberry traveled to Iraq when he was a news _____ (microphone/correspondent).

7. He interviewed _____ (journalists/refugees) in the mountains of Iraq.

8. John faced some challenges because he became _____ (diverse/paralyzed).

9. He has had an exciting _____ (career/correspondent).

Reread

> When you read aloud, pay attention to the punctuation. Think about the meaning of the group of words between punctuation marks. Remember to pause briefly at commas and pause a little longer at periods, question marks, and exclamation points.

▶ In the passage below, underline commas and circle the end punctuation. This will help you know when to pause. With a partner, take turns reading aloud the passage. The first sentence has been marked for you.

    Later that year, John got a chance to become a news reporter. This was very exciting, but John was worried. Would he be able to get around well enough to follow a story? John fixed his wheelchair with special parts. Sometimes he would have to be in places with rough roads or no sidewalks. John used special tires and made steel plates that protected the wheel gears. He learned to be ready for anything.

    John soon had a job as a news correspondent for National Public Radio. This job included traveling to the Middle East and interviewing leaders of countries, but John also talked with ordinary people. He felt it was part of his job to let his audience hear those voices.

Writing

Extend and Write

▶ What kind of person is John Hockenberry? What are some things he does? Use the chart to list facts about him.

John Hockenberry	
Career	Interests

▶ Now use the facts you listed to write one or two paragraphs to describe John Hockenberry.

Get Ready to Read

The 12-Hour Race

1 Characters

 **Gina** a member of Bike Builders

 **Joey** a bike team member

 **Eva** Gina's best friend

 **Mr. Lo** a teacher at Gina's school

2 Setting: Connell Park

3 Vocabulary

course path for a race

lap the entire length of a racecourse or swimming pool

volunteer work without pay

repair fix

session a meeting for a certain purpose

confidence the feeling of knowing that you can do something well

endurance the strength to go a long way

instruction teaching

pace keep moving at a steady speed

circuit the distance around a course

4 Build Background

- What do you know about bike races?
- What do bike riders do to stay safe?

Lesson 6   71

The 12-Hour Race

Gina walked up to her friends. "Hi, guys! What's up?" she asked.

"There's a 12-hour bike race at Connell Park," said Rico. "How can a bike race go on for 12 hours?"

Eva explained, "It's a team race. Five team members take turns riding the **course,** over and over, and the team that goes the most **laps** in 12 hours wins the race."

"The race will raise money for Bike Builders, too," Joey added. "You **volunteer** for them, don't you, Eva?"

"Yes, Gina and I both do, and it's a lot of fun!" Eva continued, "Bike Builders helps kids learn how to **repair** their own bikes and be safe bike riders. We have lots of bike activities."

"Joey and I have already decided to start a team," said Beth. "Why don't you three join us? You all race bikes."

Gina said, "I would if it were swimming, but I'm not into biking anymore." She quickly walked away, remembering the day last year when her bike slid out from under her during a friendly race with Eva. Gina skidded down a hill and broke her ankle that day. She still rode her bike, but she didn't race anymore.

Two days later, Gina and Eva were on their way to a bike team **session.** Eva had decided to race, and Gina would help the team keep their bikes working well.

"Don't you miss racing?" asked Eva.

Gina shook her head. "Getting hurt took the fun out of biking."

"I think you're still a bike racer," Eva declared. "I saw the gleam in your eyes when we used to race. You've just lost your **confidence.**"

Every afternoon the team met at Connell Park, where they worked on improving their **endurance** by biking the three-mile-long trail that ran through the park.

Mr. Lo, their teacher, had agreed to coach the team. He started each session with bike safety **instruction.**

"If you feel the bike starting to slip, just relax," he said. "Lean into the fall, put your foot out, and then you can just set the bike on its side without getting hurt."

Gina was listening as she put together the kits to repair the riders' bikes, and she thought, "That makes sense. I should have done that when I fell."

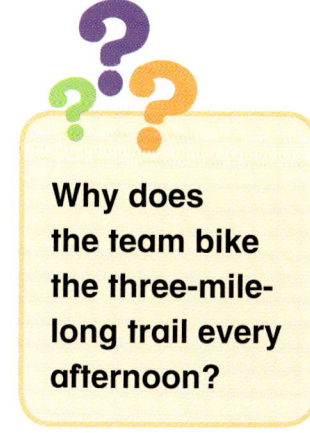

Why does the team bike the three-mile-long trail every afternoon?

A week before the race, Joey was not at practice.

"Where is Joey? We need him!" Eva exclaimed. "He's the strongest member of the team."

Just then, Joey limped across the grass on crutches. The team gathered around him, asking, "What happened to you?"

"I slipped while I was taking out the trash," Joey said with a frown, "and I twisted my knee."

The group groaned. "What do we do now?" asked Eva.

Mr. Lo said, "Don't worry, Joey. We'll work it out."

"Could Joey and I trade places?" Gina's voice came from behind Eva's bike. "If you can repair the bikes, I'll take over your spot on the team, Joey."

"Are you sure, Gina?" asked Mr. Lo. "You haven't been training with us."

"I've worked on my endurance by swimming laps at the pool every morning," said Gina. "Besides, I haven't completely given up my bike."

"All right!" "Go, Gina!" "This will be awesome." The excited team members all spoke at once.

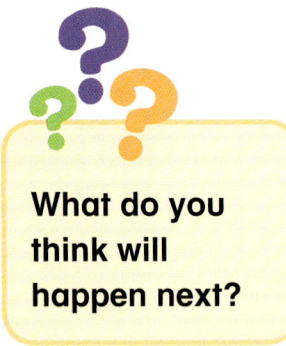

What do you think will happen next?

The day of the race finally arrived. The team gathered under their tent, setting up their gear. There were stands with water and snacks ready to grab and hand to racers as they rode by.

Mr. Lo called the team together. "Remember, this race is a team effort. A single racer can't win it alone. **Pace** yourself and make as many laps as you can. Don't forget to take one hill at a time, one pedal at a time. When you get tired, stop and let the next team member take over. That is the way to get the most out of your race."

The first racers from each team lined up along the starting line. The announcer began to speak. "This race is 12 hours long, and the team that rides the most laps will raise the most money for Bike Builders. It is now 7:00 A.M. I will blow the horn at 7:00 P.M. The sound of the horn means the race is over. Good luck for the next 12 hours!" The flag waved and the beginning bikers burst across the starting line.

Gina's legs were pumping up and down, and she was full of confidence. Her team had settled into a fast but comfortable speed, and everyone was having fun.

Now it was 6:15 P.M., and the race was almost over. Gina had made four **circuits** of the course during the day. She felt as if she had never stopped racing. This would be her final circuit, and she was a little tired, but she still had enough energy left to finish this lap easily. She coasted down a steep hill.

Suddenly, Gina's bike started to slide. She panicked and grabbed the handlebars tightly. Then she remembered Mr. Lo saying, "Just relax. Lean into the fall." Gina took a deep breath and relaxed. She slid down a small slope. Her legs were scratched, and her hands were shaking.

"It's okay," she whispered to herself. "You're almost there. You can make it." Gina climbed back on the bike and rode down the path.

When Gina reached the team tent, her team members, who were sprawled out on the lawn, gave a weak cheer. "I know everyone is tired," said Mr. Lo. "We've done a great job, but one more lap could put us in the lead. Who can do it?"

Gina was just about to say no, but she looked at her teammates, who had all worked so hard. Then she remembered the kids who had bikes that were in good shape because she volunteered for Bike Builders. "Sure, I'll do it," she said.

Gina grabbed a water bottle and took a drink. Then she headed down the path one more time. Her legs were tired and shaky from the fall. It wasn't hard to pace herself on the flat stretches, but the hills were a struggle.

Finally, Gina came to the last big hill. She felt worn out, her scratched legs hurt, and her bike wobbled. "I'm going to let everyone down," she thought.

Then Gina remembered Mr. Lo's instruction. "One hill at a time, one pedal at a time," she thought. "This is for Bike Builders and for the team."

Gina strained up the hill and then sped down with a shout. At the finish line ahead, she saw a big banner made by the Bike Builders kids, saying, "Thanks for riding for us!"

"I'm the one who should say thanks!" Gina said with a grin as she zoomed across the finish line.

Why did Gina agree to do another lap?

Comprehension

Summarizing

When you summarize what you have read, you tell what happens in the story.

▶ List the most important ideas in each paragraph below. Then summarize the passage.

1. Suddenly, Gina's bike started to slide. She panicked and grabbed the handlebars tightly. Then she remembered Mr. Lo saying, "Just relax. Lean into the fall." Gina took a deep breath and relaxed. She slid down a small slope. Her legs were scratched, and her hands were shaking.

2. "It's okay," she whispered to herself. "You're almost there." Gina climbed back on the bike and rode down the path.

Important Ideas	
Paragraph 1	Gina scared, slides down slope
Paragraph 2	

Summary _____

Summarizing

Comprehension

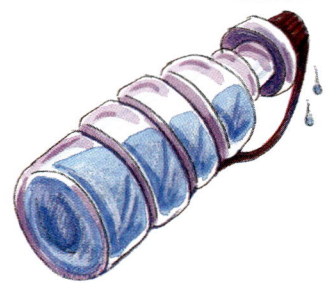

▶ Think about the story "The 12-Hour Race." Write the most important things that happened at the beginning, middle, and end of the story. Then write a summary of the story.

Beginning

Middle

End

Summary

Word Study

Pronouns

Pronouns are words that stand for nouns. They are words such as *I, you, it, we,* and *they.*
Jim is a good rider. He rides up and down many hills quickly.

▶ Write the correct pronoun to complete each item below. The pronoun should stand for the underlined word or words.

1. Colin and I love to ride bikes. _____ ride nearly every day.

2. Dad likes to ride, too. _____ took a class in mountain biking.

3. The big race is coming up. _____ will be next week.

4. Those riders are very good. _____ might win the race.

5. Julie is their team captain. _____ is also the fastest rider on their team.

6. Julie and Jim are good friends. _____ often practice racing together.

7. Jim's mother checks their endurance. _____ uses a stopwatch to time them.

8. When they complete the circuit, she gives them water. _____ tastes especially good on a hot day.

80 Lesson 6 • Word Study: Subject Pronouns

Words to Learn

> Read the words in the box. Write the word that answers each riddle.

course   lap   session   endurance

1. I am a meeting for a purpose. _____
2. I am the path for the race. _____
3. I am one length of the bicycle path. _____
4. I am the strength you need to finish the race. _____

> Read the words in the box. Write the word that completes each sentence.

| instruction   pace   confidence |
volunteer   repair   circuit

1. Gina's first plan was to help _____ bikes at the race.
2. "I can do that because I _____ at Bike Builders," she thought.
3. The racers made a complete _____ of the bike trail.
4. Gina remembered to _____ herself to stay strong till the end.
5. She was glad she had listened to Mr. Lo's _____.
6. Finally, she had enough _____ to ride in the race.

Fluency

Reread

> When you read characters' conversations aloud, remember to read with expression. Think about how each character would say his or her statements in the story.

▶ With a partner, read the passage below, taking turns with each character's words.

Two days later, Gina and Eva were on their way to a bike team session. Eva had decided to race, and Gina would help the team keep their bikes working well.

"Don't you miss riding?" asked Eva.

Gina shook her head. "Getting hurt took the fun out of biking."

"I think you're still a bike racer," Eva declared. "I saw the gleam in your eyes when we used to race. You've just lost your confidence."

Every afternoon, the team met at Connell Park, where they worked on improving their endurance by biking the three-mile-long trail that ran through the park.

Mr. Lo, their teacher, had agreed to coach the team. He started each session with bike safety instruction.

"If you feel the bike starting to slip, just relax," he said. "Lean into the fall, put your foot out, and then you can just set the bike on its side without getting hurt."

Writing

Extend and Write

▶ Gina gained confidence as she began racing again. Think about how you gained confidence in something you have learned to do well. Make notes in the box.

Notes	
What I learned to do well	**How I became confident in doing it**
_____	_____
_____	_____
_____	_____

▶ Now summarize what you did to become better at what you did.

Writing • Lesson 6   83

7

Get Ready to Read
A Gray Day in May

1 Topic

Mount St. Helens volcano

2 Vocabulary

erupt	suddenly force out steam and lava
spew	spit out with force
unusual	not what you would expect
magma	hot, melted rock
toxic	poisonous
renew	make like new again
nutrient	something that is needed by living things
enriched	improved
flourish	to grow well

3 Build Background

- What happens when a volcano erupts?
- How might people, animals, and plants be affected by a volcano?

A Gray Day in May

It began as a nice spring day in Spokane, Washington, on May 18, 1980. The sun was warm, and the trees were starting to bud. Halfway through an outdoor party in the middle of that lovely day, a friend came up to me.

"Did you hear the news?" she asked. "Mount St. Helens **erupted!**"

A Faraway Mountain

I knew a little about Mount St. Helens, but not much. I had heard that the mountain had started **spewing** smoke and fire a few days earlier. That was **unusual**, but I didn't really think about it. No one did. Many people in Spokane must have had the same thought I had: "A volcano couldn't erupt in America. Things like that only happen in other places."

Even when I heard what had happened, I didn't worry. The mountain was nearly 300 miles from Spokane. What could possibly happen to us here?

An ash cloud similar to the one that reached Spokane, Washington, in May 1980

Darkness at Noon

I soon found out what could happen! The sky got darker and darker. Even though it was noon, it looked like twilight, when the sun goes down.

People at the party started to walk to their cars. No one knew what to expect, but it seemed safer to go home right away.

My house was on the other side of town. As I drove down the main road, little flakes started to fall from the sky. What was that? It couldn't be snowing in May!

The flakes were ash that Mount St. Helens had spewed out. The explosion from the volcano was so strong that the ash had blown all the way to Spokane. Over the next few days, the ash cloud spread as far as 900 miles away.

What we learned later is that the ash in the air was made of tiny bits of exploded rock and **magma.** The heat had burned the rock into a fine, dusty ash. At the time, though, the flakes did look like snow.

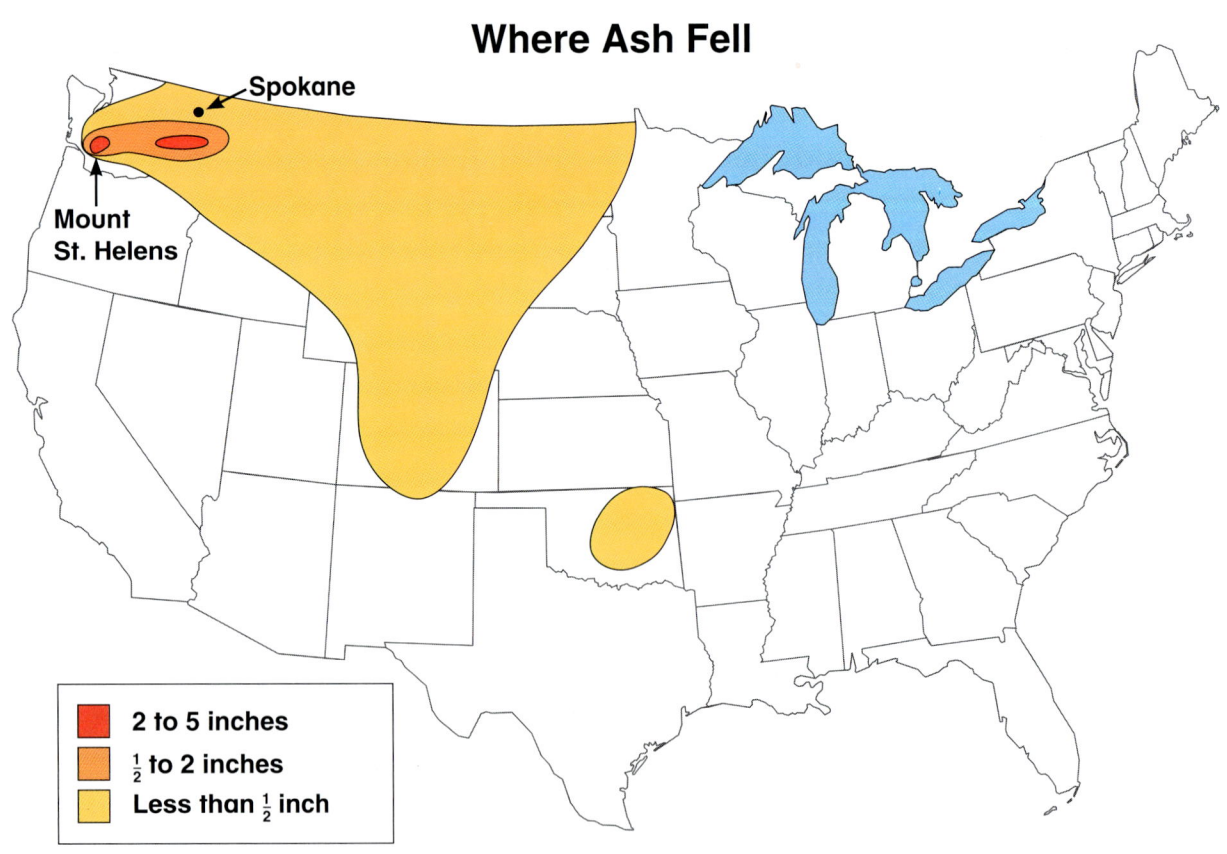

Where Ash Fell

- 2 to 5 inches
- $\frac{1}{2}$ to 2 inches
- Less than $\frac{1}{2}$ inch

A Scary Drive Home

The sky was now as dark as midnight. The streetlights had turned on, triggered by the darkness. Soon the ash flakes were falling faster. As I drove, the floating ash rushed at my windshield. My headlights shone a bright glare in my eyes as they reflected off the ash. This made it almost impossible to see the road for more than a few feet ahead of the car. It reminded me of driving through a blizzard.

The ash was slick, too. The car swerved, so I had to drive slowly. I could see other cars stranded by the side of the road. I approached a stop sign. My car skidded when I stepped on the brakes. I decided to just keep moving so that I wouldn't hit anything or get stuck on the road.

A drive that usually took twenty minutes took more than two hours! The tires spun and the car slid backwards a bit as I inched up my steep driveway. At last, I made it home.

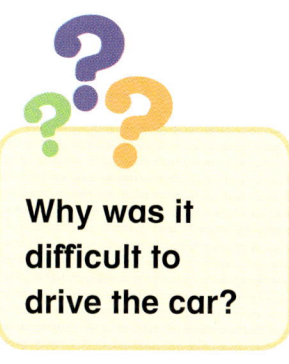

Why was it difficult to drive the car?

People trying to drive on ash-covered streets

The Day After

The next day, everyone stayed indoors. Two inches of ash from the volcano had covered the whole city. The day was very warm, but it looked like it had snowed outside. Officials warned us not to go out.

For a few days, schools and many businesses were closed. After that, I went back to my job teaching school. The students had to stay indoors at first because some scientists thought that the ash might be **toxic.** My class got very tired of having recess inside!

The scientists worked fast, testing the ash to see whether it would be toxic to people's skin or eyes. I heard reports of one bold scientist who decided to save time. He rubbed some ash on his skin, and he found that it did not burn. After more tests, people were told that they could go outside.

It was unclear whether the ash would harm people's lungs, but at least it was no longer floating in the air. Everyone had to wear facemasks to go outside. The masks would help protect our lungs in case the ash turned out to be dangerous. The masks were uncomfortable, but we had no choice.

A man cleaning ash off cars after the Mount St. Helens eruption

Things Go Wrong

The streets of the city were empty. Here and there, people walked along with their faces covered. Everything had come to a stop.

The next day, my neighbor's car started smoking when he tried to drive it. The ash had clogged the valves in the engine so it stopped. This happened to cars and buses all over town! I did not drive my car again until some of the ash had been cleared from the roads.

The ash itself was a strange substance. When it was dry, it sent up powdery clouds. When the ash got wet, it turned into something like cement. Some people tried to wash it down the street drains. The wet ash blocked sewer lines all over town!

Other unusual things happened. Many people in Spokane got requests from their friends to send samples of Mount St. Helens ash. The ash clogged the machines at the post office as the envelopes went through the machines. It took weeks to clean the machines out.

The Mount St. Helens ash fall showed me what could happen to a city during a natural disaster.

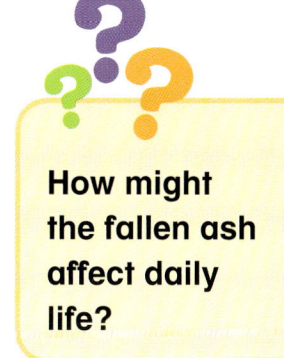

How might the fallen ash affect daily life?

People in central Washington removing ash from the streets where they lived

A Changing Landscape

How could the city **renew** itself? The ash had covered everything and stopped traffic. First, the city bulldozed the ash off the streets so people could drive.

For months afterward, the gray landscape around Spokane made it look like a city on the moon. A light coat of ash still covered the streets and buildings. The ash got on our shoes and our clothes. Plants grew, but their leaves were coated with ash. The trees and flowers looked unreal.

Scientists told us that someday the ash would make Spokane even greener and more beautiful. The ash had many **nutrients** that would gradually break down and become part of the soil. The **enriched** soil would help plants **flourish** in farms, gardens, and parks.

Over time, Spokane, and other cities that were in the path of the ash cloud, were renewed. Spokane is once again beautiful. At the time, though, it seemed that our city would be gray forever. The next year, a student wrote an essay about the eruption. It was called "My Gray Summer." No one who was there will ever forget that gray day in May.

Flower growing through ash (above) and recent photo of Spokane, Washington (right)

Comprehension

Context Clues

> When you read, you may see a word that is easy to pronounce, but you may not know what it means. Look for synonyms or other words around the word to help you figure out what it means. These words are called context clues.

▶ **Read the passage below. Then use context clues to answer the questions.**

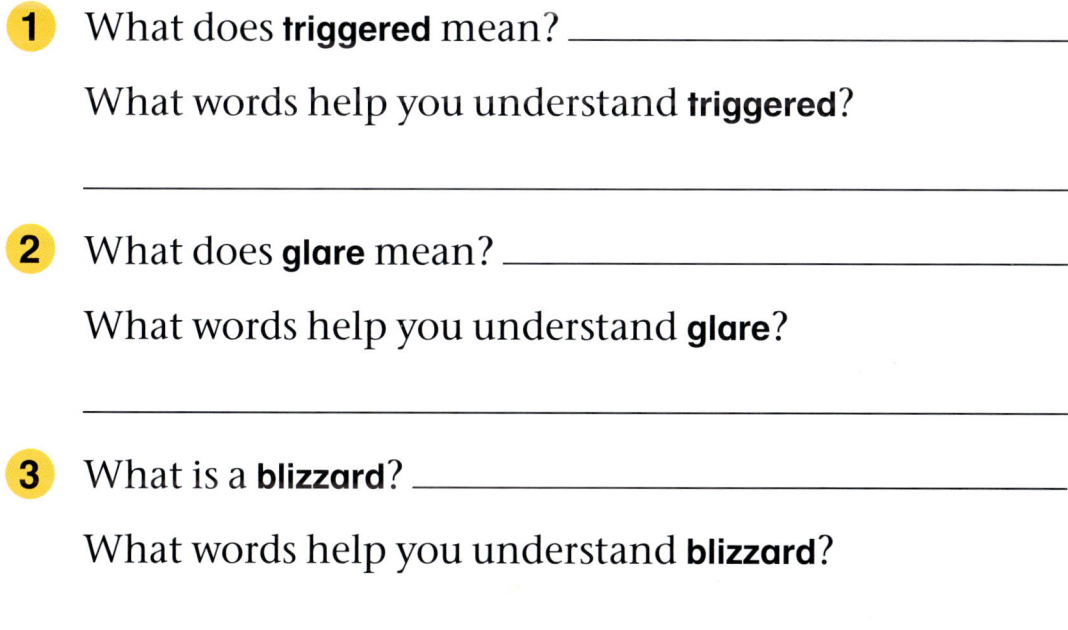

The sky was now as dark as midnight. The streetlights had turned on, <u>triggered</u> by the darkness. Soon the ash flakes were falling faster. As I drove, the floating ash rushed at my windshield. My headlights shone a bright <u>glare</u> in my eyes as they reflected off the ash. This made it almost impossible to see the road for more than a few feet ahead of the car. It reminded me of driving through a <u>blizzard</u>.

1 What does **triggered** mean? _____

What words help you understand **triggered**?

_____

2 What does **glare** mean? _____

What words help you understand **glare**?

_____

3 What is a **blizzard**? _____

What words help you understand **blizzard**?

_____

Comprehension: Context Clues • Lesson 7 **91**

Comprehension

Context Clues

▶ **Read the passage.**

The First Day Out

It had been two weeks since the ash fell, and for the first time we could go outside for recess. Our parents wouldn't let us play outside, either, and life had become very <u>tedious</u>. Staying indoors all the time was really boring!

We all had to put on our facemasks for <u>protection</u>. "Your safety is very important!" said the teacher. The mask made my face sweat, and I was very uncomfortable. I could stand the <u>discomfort</u>, though, if it meant I could run around and play a game of baseball!

▶ **Write the meaning of each word. Then write your own sentence using the word correctly.**

	Word	Meaning
1	tedious	_____

Sentence: _____

_____

2	protection	_____

Sentence: _____

_____

3	discomfort	_____

Sentence: _____

_____

92 Lesson 7 • Comprehension: Context Clues

Word Study

Prefixes: *re* and *un*

> **Prefixes such as *re* and *un* can be added to the beginnings of words to make new words.**
> re + write = rewrite   write over again
> un + clear = unclear   not clear

▶ Read each meaning. Write a word that starts with *re* or *un* to match the meaning given.

1. not like   _____
2. grow again   _____
3. tell again   _____
4. not safe   _____
5. wash again   _____
6. not real   _____

▶ Use the words you wrote above to complete the sentences.

1. People like to _____ the story of the volcano.
2. We wore facemasks because the ash might be _____.
3. After we played outside, we had to _____ our clothes.
4. The plants covered in ash looked _____.
5. They were _____ anything we had ever seen.
6. Would the plants ever _____?

Vocabulary

Words to Learn

unusual	erupt	spew	enriched	nutrient
flourish	magma	toxic	renew	

▶ **Read the words in the box. Write the word that completes each sentence.**

1. The explosion made the volcano _____ out smoke and ash.

2. A hot flow of _____ poured from the volcano.

3. A huge force from underground had caused the volcano to _____.

4. The mountain's explosion was a very _____ sight.

5. Would the ash be _____ to animals and humans? No one really knew.

6. We did know that someday the ash would _____ the soil.

7. One _____ that came from the ash and helped plants grow is nitrogen.

8. Now many plants _____ in the _____ soil.

Reread

> When you read aloud, try to read at the same speed you would when you talk. If you have trouble reading any of the words, practice them before you read the passage again.

With a small group, take turns reading the paragraphs of the passage out loud. After one person reads a paragraph, stop and retell what happened. Then continue in the same way with the other paragraphs in the passage. Remember to read at the same speed you would when you talk. Practice words that you might have trouble pronouncing.

For months afterward, the gray landscape around Spokane made it look like a city on the moon. A light coat of ash still covered the streets and buildings. The ash got on our shoes and our clothes. Plants grew, but their leaves were coated with ash. The trees and flowers looked unreal.

Scientists told us that someday the ash would make Spokane even greener and more beautiful. The ash had many nutrients that would gradually break down and become part of the soil. The enriched soil would help plants flourish in farms, gardens, and parks.

Over time, Spokane, and other cities that were in the path of the ash cloud, were renewed. Spokane is once again beautiful. At the time, though, it seemed that our city would be gray forever. The next year, a student wrote an essay about the eruption. It was called "My Gray Summer." No one who was there will ever forget that gray day in May.

Writing

Extend and Write

You think your friend would be interested in the article "A Gray Day in May." List the most interesting events of the eruption.

▶ Use the details to write an e-mail to persuade your friend to read the article.

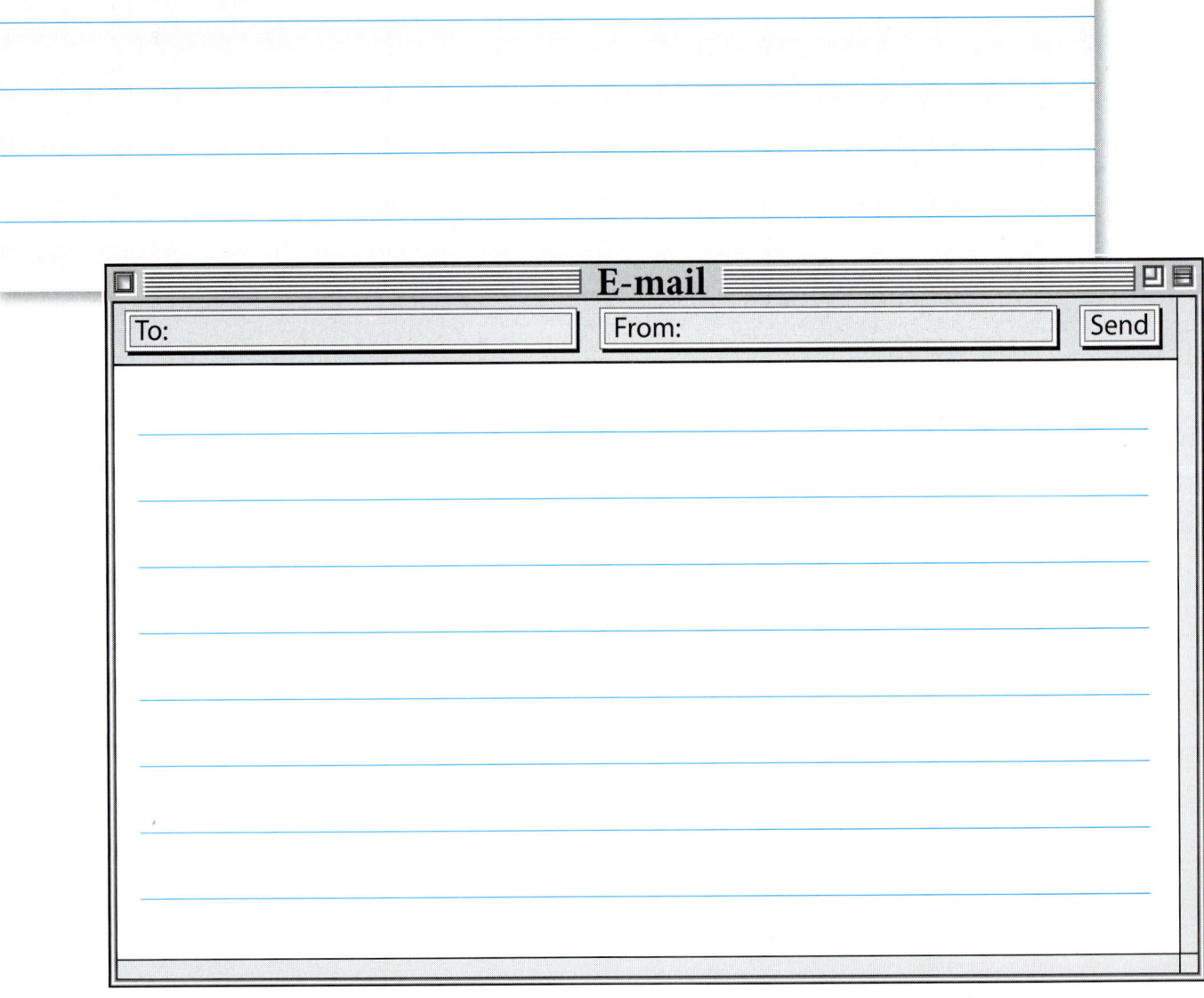

96 Lesson 7 • Writing

Get Ready to Read
Plastic Fashion

1 Topic

recycling plastic bottles

2 Vocabulary

careless not caring about results

landfill a place where trash is dumped

resourceful able to solve problems

fabric cloth

fleece a soft, warm fabric

fiber a thread-like material

organic from things that were once alive

blend a combination of two or more things

3 Build Background

- What objects made of plastic do people recycle?
- How is recycled plastic used?

Plastic Fashion

Stop and think about how many plastic water or soda bottles your family uses in a week. Do you use five? Ten? More than ten? Do you put them in a recycling bin or just toss them in the trash?

Water bottles are the most recycled plastic items in the United States. Along with other recyclable plastics, these water bottles are sent to recycling centers to be sorted.

The plastic used to make water and soda bottles is easier to recycle than some other plastics. It can be used to make many other items. This symbol ♳ tells how likely it is that each kind of plastic can be recycled. Here is a guide for recycling plastic:

 easy to recycle    fairly easy to recycle

 more difficult to recycle    very difficult to recycle

Empty plastic bottles

The Problem with Plastic

People are recycling more now than ever before. In recent years, more than a third of the millions of plastic soda bottles in the United States are recycled. That sounds good, but it could be better. Nearly half of all paper products and more than half of all aluminum cans are recycled. Besides, if one-third of soda bottles are recycled, that means that two-thirds are not!

Why are Americans not recycling all of the millions of soda and water bottles they use each year? Often people get **careless** and forget to put their bottles in a recycling bin. These bottles end up in **landfills.** Because the plastic does not decay, the landfills take over more and more land.

Also, many people are careless about the kind of plastic they put in recycling bins. Remember that not all plastic is easy to recycle. The bad news is that just one item with the wrong symbol can ruin a whole batch of recycled plastic. The good news is that soda and water bottles are usually made from type 1 plastic.

Plastic Soft Drink Bottles

Recycled / Not recycled

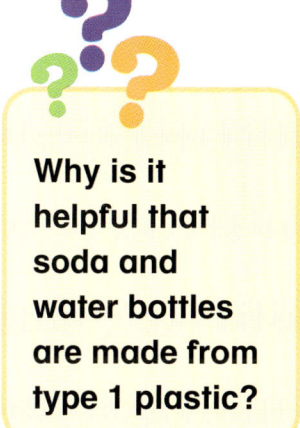

Why is it helpful that soda and water bottles are made from type 1 plastic?

Plastic bottles ready to be recycled

Even the bottles put in recycling bins may not get recycled. More and more plastic is piling up at recycling centers, mainly because there are not enough companies who want to use that plastic. The demand for recycled plastic is not as high as the number of water and soda bottles that are used each year.

Girls wearing fleece hats made from recycled plastic

A Cool Solution

Today, some **resourceful** companies are trying to make a difference by manufacturing clothes out of recycled plastic. One **fabric** that can be made from plastic is **fleece.** Fleece is a soft, fuzzy fabric that can trap heat. It is used for warm clothes such as hats, jackets, scarves, and gloves.

The plastic comes from recycled water and soda bottles. The bottles are cut into narrow strips and then melted. The melted plastic is spun into a **fiber** that makes a very thick fabric called "bottle fleece." Yarn made from recycled plastic is soft and smooth like yarns made from **organic** materials such as wool or cotton.

Other fabrics can also be made by using plastic. Some companies make T-shirts from a **blend** of 50% recycled plastic and 50% recycled cotton. The T-shirts are soft and comfortable, and they look great.

Some companies have found other creative ways to reuse materials. One resourceful company doesn't throw anything away! Shipments of recycled plastic come to the company in large cardboard boxes. The company reuses those boxes to send out its fleece products. All of the fleece scraps left-over from making its hats are tied into big bundles and sent to schools or art groups to use in art projects.

The company also puts its kitchen waste, such as coffee grounds or old bread, in a pile with other organic materials. There the waste materials turn into compost, a mixture that is added to soil to enrich it. The compost is then used in a company vegetable garden.

The company's owner proudly announced, "I finally had to cancel our garbage service!"

Why do you think the company's owner canceled the garbage service?

A compost bin

More Plastic You Can Wear

There are other stylish things to wear and carry to school that are made from recycled plastic. Besides fleece, plastic can also be spun into fibers for strong fabrics that are used for making backpacks, baseball caps, and lunch bags. Some are made totally of recycled plastic and others are a blend.

Believe it or not, plastic fashions are everywhere. Look for labels that say "Made with Recycled Materials" when you are shopping. Think about how many bottles do not go into landfills when they are being recycled into fabric. The chart below shows how many bottles are used for each piece of plastic fashion. Bottles equal clothing!

Facts for Thoughtful Shoppers

One 2-liter water or soda bottle = one fleece hat

Five 2-liter water or soda bottles = one extra-large T-shirt

Twenty-five 2-liter water or soda bottles = one jacket

Shopping bag made of recycled plastic

What Else Can Be Made?

More and more companies are experimenting with new ways to use recycled plastic in their products. The number of companies using recycled plastic has tripled in the last ten years.

Today, you can ride on a recycled plastic wakeboard or use a bike rack made of recycled plastic to carry your bike. You can even paddle down a river in a kayak made of recycled plastic.

If you like buying recycled plastic products, write to the companies that make them. These companies like to hear from their customers. If they know that you support their work, they will make more products from recycled plastic. Plastic is already a part of your everyday life, and recycled plastic can be a part of your future. Just think, you can look and feel good while you keep plastic out of landfills!

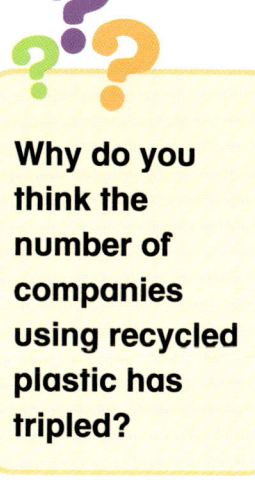

Why do you think the number of companies using recycled plastic has tripled?

A kayak made of recycled plastic

Comprehension

Making Inferences

Sometimes when you read, you have to use facts in the article and what you already know to make inferences, or logical guesses, about the topic.

▶ **Read this paragraph.**

People are recycling more now than ever before. In recent years, more than a third of the millions of plastic soda bottles in the United States are recycled. That sounds good, but it could be better. Nearly half of all paper products and more than half of all aluminum cans are recycled. Besides, if one-third of soda bottles are recycled, that means that two-thirds are not!

▶ **Which of these statements is an inference you could make from the paragraph? Circle it.**

a. People recycle the same amount of plastic bottles and aluminum cans.

b. More plastic bottles could be recycled in the United States.

c. Plastic bottles are hard to recycle.

▶ **List two facts in the paragraph that help you make this inference.**

1 _____

2 _____

Comprehension

Making Inferences

▶ **Read the following paragraphs. Circle the inference you could make from each paragraph.**

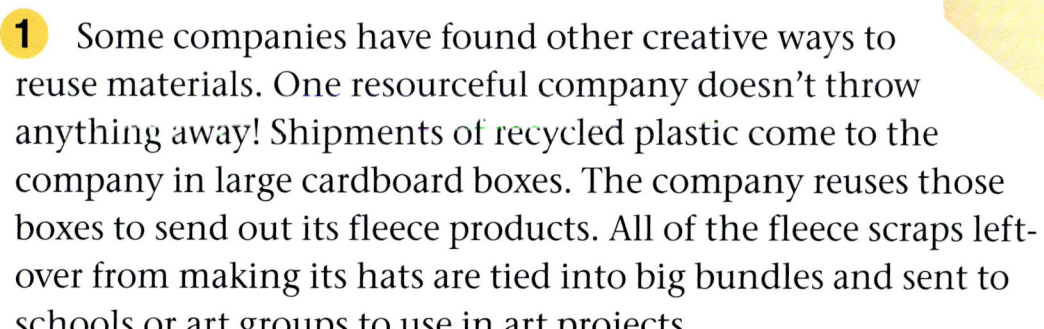

1 Some companies have found other creative ways to reuse materials. One resourceful company doesn't throw anything away! Shipments of recycled plastic come to the company in large cardboard boxes. The company reuses those boxes to send out its fleece products. All of the fleece scraps leftover from making its hats are tied into big bundles and sent to schools or art groups to use in art projects.

a. The company stores leftover scraps in shipping boxes.

b. The company makes boxes.

c. Recycling and reusing materials are important to the company.

2 The company also puts its kitchen waste, such as coffee grounds or old bread, in a pile with other organic materials. There the waste materials turn into compost, a mixture that is added to soil to enrich it. The compost is then used in a company vegetable garden.

a. The company produces and sells compost.

b. Compost is helpful in growing vegetables.

c. Coffee grounds poison growing plants.

▶ **What can you infer about what the company might do with the cans from its vending machines?**

_____

_____

_____

Comprehension: Making Inferences • Lesson 8

Word Study

Suffixes: *less, ful, able*

The suffix *less* added to the end of a word means "without."
care + less = careless   without care
Some people are careless about what they do with plastic bottles.

The suffix *ful* means "full of."
thought + ful = thoughtful   full of thoughts
Thoughtful people are often careful, too.

The suffix *able* means "providing" or "able to be."
break + able = breakable   able to be broken
Glass bottles are breakable.

▶ Write a word with *less*, *ful*, or *able* for each clue. Then use the word in a sentence that shows the meaning of the word. The first one has been done for you.

1 without leaves   _leafless_
Those trees are leafless in winter.

2 full of play _____

_____

3 without a name _____

_____

4 providing comfort _____

_____

5 able to be read _____

_____

6 full of power _____

_____

106   Lesson 8 • Word Study: Suffixes: *less, ful, able*

Words to Learn

▶ Read the words in the box. Write the word that solves each riddle.

| careless | landfill | resourceful | fabric |
| fleece | fiber | organic | blend |

1. This is something warm and fuzzy. _____
2. This is made of two or more things. _____
3. This can be made into cloth. _____
4. Shirts are made of this. _____
5. People who are like this come up with smart plans. _____
6. People who are like this don't think about their actions. _____
7. This is where trash goes. _____
8. This is made of things from nature. _____

Vocabulary • Lesson 8 107

Fluency

Reread

> When you read aloud, try to read at the same speed you would when you talk. If you have trouble reading any of the words, practice them before you read the passage again.

▶ With a partner, read the passage aloud at a steady rate.

What Else Can Be Made?

More and more companies are experimenting with new ways to use recycled plastic in their products. The number of companies using recycled plastic has tripled in the last ten years.

Today, you can ride on a recycled plastic wakeboard or use a bike rack made of recycled plastic to carry your bike. You can even paddle down a river in a kayak made of recycled plastic.

If you like buying recycled plastic products, write to the companies that make them. These companies like to hear from their customers. If they know that you support their work, they will make more products from recycled plastic. Plastic is already a part of your everyday life, and recycled plastic can be a part of your future. Just think, you can look and feel good while you keep plastic out of landfills!

Extend and Write

▶ One company in the article sends its fleece scraps to schools to be used in art projects. Think about something you know how to make or do that reuses something. List the materials you would use. Then write a paragraph that explains the steps you would follow.

Materials

Writing • Lesson 8 109

Review

Maisie's Pool

Maisie DeVore sat on the edge of the swimming pool and dipped her toes into the water. Sarah and Alex splashed nearby. Kansas had been hit by a heat wave.

"It sure is hot today!" noted Sarah. "What would we do without this pool?"

"I don't know," said Alex. "How did a small town like ours ever get money for a swimming pool?"

"Cans," Maisie said. The children were puzzled.

"I decided 35 years ago that our town needed a pool," she explained. "So I started recycling cans to raise money. I hunted for them constantly. I found cans along roads and picked them up at picnics. Most people predicted that I would fail. However, I had confidence in myself."

"After a while, people started to help," Maisie went on. "People left bags of cans on my porch. The school had a can-collecting contest, which really encouraged me. Thirty years of hard work paid off. In 2001, the pool was finally built."

"Once the pool was open, it seemed as though every journalist in the state wanted to talk to me. I even received an award in Washington, D.C."

Maisie smiled.

"All of that was fantastic, but seeing my friends and neighbors swimming is the best reward of all."

Review

▶ **Read the questions. Then fill in the circle next to the best answer.**

1 Why did Maisie want a pool for her town?
- Ⓐ The high school needed a pool for swim meets.
- Ⓑ She wanted to be famous.
- Ⓒ Her friends and neighbors would enjoy the pool.
- Ⓓ She had many cans to recycle.

2 What was one effect of Maisie's hard work?
- Ⓐ She received an award in Washington, D.C.
- Ⓑ She became a member of the city council.
- Ⓒ She lost confidence in herself.
- Ⓓ She predicted she would be famous.

3 Which detail tells you one way other people helped Maisie reach her goal?
- Ⓐ People went swimming in the pool.
- Ⓑ Every journalist in the state wanted to talk to her.
- Ⓒ Maisie picked up cans along roads.
- Ⓓ The school held a can-collecting contest.

4 Which statement is a good summary of the story?
- Ⓐ Sarah and Alex enjoyed swimming in the pool.
- Ⓑ Maisie raised money from recycling cans to pay for a pool.
- Ⓒ Maisie built a factory to recycle cans in her town.
- Ⓓ Maisie had a wonderful vacation in Washington, D.C.

Review

5 In this story, what does **puzzled** mean?
- Ⓐ sure
- Ⓑ confused
- Ⓒ happy
- Ⓓ hot

6 In this story, what does **constantly** mean?
- Ⓐ never
- Ⓑ quietly
- Ⓒ everywhere
- Ⓓ all the time

7 Which word describes how Maisie felt about being able to build a pool in her hometown?
- Ⓐ careless
- Ⓑ helpless
- Ⓒ hopeful
- Ⓓ boastful

8 Which word shows more than one?
- Ⓐ friend's
- Ⓑ Kansas
- Ⓒ his
- Ⓓ children

9 Sarah and Alex went swimming. _____ asked Maisie about the pool.
- Ⓐ We
- Ⓑ They
- Ⓒ She
- Ⓓ You

Homes of Grass and Dirt

About 150 years ago, people moved west to the flat land in the middle of the country. Few tall trees grew in this environment. These newcomers could not build their homes from wood. So they became resourceful and used a material called sod. Sod is dirt held together by grass roots.

To build their sod homes, people dug the sod out of the ground. A special plow cut through the soil to produce sod "bricks." A good time to cut sod was after a rain, when the roots were soft.

Builders placed the bricks to form a wall about two feet thick. They left space for doors and a few small windows. The roofs were made in different ways. Some were made from twigs and branches. Other roofs had sod bricks held up by a large log or beam. Fancier ceilings were covered with fabric to catch any dirt that crumbled.

Like homes of today, sod houses helped keep out the summer heat and winter cold. However, the homes also had many problems. On rainy days, water sometimes leaked in. Bugs and mice often scurried through the walls into the house. Imagine trying to keep a sod house clean! It's no wonder that people don't live in such unusual homes today.

Review

▶ **Read the questions. Then fill in the circle next to the best answer.**

1 What is the main idea of the article?
- Ⓐ how sod houses were built
- Ⓑ how sod is grown
- Ⓒ how sod house roofs were different
- Ⓓ where to find sod houses today

2 Which detail tells why people did not use wood to build houses?
- Ⓐ Some roofs used sod bricks.
- Ⓑ A good time to cut sod was after a rain.
- Ⓒ Few tall trees grew in this environment.
- Ⓓ A home built of sod was not easy to keep clean.

3 What words help you understand the meaning of **beam** in the article?
- Ⓐ summer heat and winter cold
- Ⓑ large log
- Ⓒ fancier ceilings
- Ⓓ dirt that crumbled

4 In which way is a sod home like most homes today?
- Ⓐ They both help protect from the heat and cold.
- Ⓑ They both have walls that can easily be painted.
- Ⓒ They both have dirt ceilings.
- Ⓓ They both have roofs made of twigs.

Review

5 In this article, what does the word **resourceful** mean?
  Ⓐ able to move quickly
  Ⓑ willing to help
  Ⓒ able to solve problems
  Ⓓ unable to build

6 In this article, what does the word **crumbled** mean?
  Ⓐ built up
  Ⓑ melted
  Ⓒ came together
  Ⓓ broke into small pieces

7 Which word is a synonym for **build**?
  Ⓐ move
  Ⓑ construct
  Ⓒ destroy
  Ⓓ paint

8 People began _____ west to live on the flat land in the middle of the country.
  Ⓐ move
  Ⓑ moved
  Ⓒ moving
  Ⓓ will move

9 Which meaning of **flat** is used in this article?
  Ⓐ not shiny
  Ⓑ smooth and level
  Ⓒ off pitch
  Ⓓ with very little air

Glossary

Aa

amaze (uh-MAYZ) *verb* surprise very much

anxious (ANGK-shus) *adjective* worried

astonished (uh-STON-isht) *adjective* surprised

Bb

blend (BLEND) *noun* a combination of two or more things

Cc

career (kuh-REER) *noun* person's job or series of jobs through life

careless (KAYR-les) *adjective* not caring about results

circuit (SUR-kut) *noun* the distance around a course

confidence (KON-fi-dens) *noun* the feeling of knowing that you can do something well

constantly (KON-stunt-lee) *adverb* all the time

contest (KON-test) *noun* a game between two people or teams to win

correspondent (kor-uh-SPON-dunt) *noun* journalist who travels to report a story

course (KORS) *noun* path for a race

crumble (KRUM-bul) *verb* break into small pieces

Dd

damage (DAM-ij) *noun* loss or harm

dangerous (DAYN-jur-us) *adjective* causing harm

diverse (dy-VURS) *adjective* different

dribble (DRIB-ul) *verb* move a ball forward by bouncing it

116 Glossary

Ee

eager (EE-gur) *adjective* wanting to do something

earthquake (URTH-kwayk) *noun* a very hard shaking of the ground

edit (ED-it) *verb* make spoken or written words more clear

encourage (en-KUR-ij) *verb* gently push someone to do something

endurance (en-DUR-uns) *noun* the strength to go a long way

enriched (en-RICHT) *adjective* improved

environment (en-VY-run-munt) *noun* the setting where something lives

errand (AYR-und) *noun* a short trip to do something

erupt (ih-RUPT) *verb* suddenly force out steam and lava

expand (ek-SPAND) *verb* make bigger

Ff

fabric (FAB-rik) *noun* cloth

fantastic (fan-TAS-tik) *adjective* very good, wonderful

fiber (FY-bur) *noun* a thread-like material

fierce (FEERS) *adjective* able to attack; dangerous

fleece (FLEES) *noun* a soft, warm fabric

flourish (FLUR-ish) *verb* to grow well

Gg

gigantic (jy-GAN-tik) *adjective* huge, very large

grateful (GRAYT-ful) *adjective* wanting to show thanks

Hh

hesitate (HEZ-uh-tayt) *verb* pause because of feeling unsure

Ii

instruction (in-STRUK-shun) *noun* teaching

Glossary **117**

Jj

journalist (JUR-nul-ist) *noun* person who tells the news

Ll

landfill (LAND-fil) *noun* a place where trash is dumped

lap (LAP) *noun* the entire length of a racecourse or swimming pool

larva (LAR-vuh) *noun* the wormlike form of a baby beetle

Mm

magma (MAG-muh) *noun* hot, melted rock

material (muh-TEER-ee-ul) *noun* what something is used for or made from

memorize (MEM-uh-ryz) *verb* learn by heart

microphone (MY-kru-fohn) *noun* device used to send a voice to another place

Nn

newcomer (NOO-kum-ur) *noun* someone who has just come to a place

nutrient (NOO-tree-unt) *noun* something that is needed by living things

Oo

organic (or-GAN-ik) *adjective* from things that were once alive

Pp

pace (PAYS) *verb* keep moving at a steady speed

paralyzed (PAYR-uh-lyzd) *adjective* not able to move

performance (per-FOR-mens) *noun* a play or a show

predict (prih-DIKT) *verb* tell what is going to happen later

produce (pruh-DOOS) *verb* plan and write a show

puzzle (PUZ-uhl) *verb* to confuse

Rr

react (ree-AKT) *verb* do something because of what someone or something else does

refugee (ref-YOO-jee) *noun* person who must leave home because of a war

renew (ree-NOO) *verb* make like new again

repair (ree-PAYR) *verb* fix

resourceful (rih-SORS-ful) *adjective* able to solve problems

Ss

scurry (SKUR-ee) *verb* move quickly

series (SEER-eez) *noun* a group of similar things coming one after another

session (SESH-un) *noun* a meeting for a certain purpose

shoot (SHOOT) *verb* throw a ball toward a goal

spew (SPYOO) *verb* spit out with force

survivor (sur-VY-vur) *noun* person who stays alive after a harmful event

Tt

toxic (TOK-sik) *adjective* poisonous

trait (TRAYT) *noun* special feature of a person or other living thing

Uu

unique (yoo-NEEK) *adjective* different from all others

unusual (un-YOO-zhoo-ul) *adjective* not what you would expect

Vv

vibration (vy-BRAY-shun) *noun* a shaking or moving back and forth

volunteer (vol-un-TEER) *verb* work without pay